PLANNING FOR RETIREMENT

A Guide For Retirement

Steve k. Bryant

Copyright

Copyright © 2024 by **Steve k. Bryant**

All rights reserved. No part of this publication may be reproduced, distributed, or transmitted in any form or by any means, including photocopying, recording, or other electronic or mechanical methods, without the prior written permission of the publisher, except in the case of brief quotations embodied in critical reviews and certain other noncommercial uses permitted by copyright law.

Table of Contents

Introduction 10
Overview of Digital Age Retirement 10
   Retirement's Development in the Digital Age
.... 10
   The Value of Remaining Up to Date on
   Current Trends 13
   Objectives of the Guide 15
Chapter 1 19
Retirement-Related Economic Trends 19
   Market volatility and global economic trends'
   effects 23
   Strategic Financial Planning's Significance .. 26
   Strategic Financial Planning's Significance .. 30
   Management of Capital Gains 34
Chapter 2 37

Retirement Planning with Technological Advancements 37

    Digital Resources for Money Management..37

    Mobile Apps and Web Sites for seniors 39

    Improving the Retirement Experience with Technology 40

Chapter 3 42

Planning for Retirement Amidst Social and Demographic Changes.....................................42

    Extended Life Expectancy and Its Consequences 42

    Unconventional Retirement Ways of Living 43

    Accepting Non-Traditional Retirement Ways of Living 45

Chapter 4 48

In 2024, where would be the best place to retire? 48

    Top Retirement States in the United States ..48

    New International Retirement Resorts 50

Chapter 6 53

Which Month in 2024 Is Best for Retirement? 53

Benefits of Year-End Retirement for Financial Planning 53

Compiling Benefits and Taking Social Security Into Account 54

Timing of the Market and Year-End Bonuses 55

Chapter 6 57

How Much Will You Need in 2024 When You Retire? 57

Determine Retirement Requirements Using Lifestyle and Expense Data 57

The general rule is 25 times annual expenses 58

70–80% of Pre-Retirement Income to Be Replaced 58

The Value of Tailored Financial Guidance ..59

Chapter 7 61

Insurance and Health Care..............................61

Making Long-Term Care Plans 63

Chapter 8 66

Remaining Involved and Active 66

Persistent Education and Individual Development..67

Chapter 9 69

Sustaining Financial Well-Being.....................69

   Efficient Expense Management and Budgeting 69

   Keeping Your Credit Score High and Taking Care of Your Debt 72

Chapter 10 75

Mental Health and Social Connectivity............75

   Creating and Preserving Social Networks....75

   Taking Part in Community Activities............77

   Making the Most of Mental Health Resources 78

Chapter 11 82

Getting Rid of Uncertainty Around Money......82

   Techniques for Maintaining Financial Stability...82

   Emergency Savings and Preparedness 87

Chapter 12 90

Handling Medical Concerns 90

Preventive Medical Care 90

Getting Support and Resources for Healthcare
.... 92

Value of Mental Health and Overall Well-
Being.. 94

Chapter 13 98

Accepting Modifications in Lifestyle 98

Getting Used to a New Daily Schedule 98

Discovering New Interests and Purposes ... 100

Accepting Adaptability and Change 102

Chapter 14 106

Is It Time for Me to Retire? 106

Analyzing the Benefits and Drawbacks of
Early Retirement 106

Drawbacks of Early Retirement 107

The Financial Costs of Early Retirement ... 108

Recognizing the Effects of Social Security
and Pensions 109

Chapter 15 114

Advantages of Taking Early Retirement 114

Enhanced General Health and Decreased Stress Advantages for Physical Health 114

Advantages for Mental Health 115

Lifestyle Advantages 119

Chapter 16 120

Overcoming Retirement-Related Fear 120

Resolving Typical Retirement Fears 120

Fear of Losing Identity and Purpose 121

Strategies for Reducing Stress and Anxiety 122

The Theory of Unexpected Retirement (SRS) 123

Chapter 18 127

Relocating to an assisted living facility 127

Retirement Communities' Benefits 127

Retirement Community Types 129

Retirement Communities with Continuing Care (CCRCs) 130

Choosing the Ideal Community for Your Requirements Evaluating Individual 132

Requirements and Choices 132

Chapter 18 134
Maintaining Relationships with Friends and Family 134
    Techniques for Sustaining Partnerships 134
    Creating New Social Networks and Friends 135
    Technology-Assisted Staying In Touch 137

Chapter 19 141
Participating in Community Service 141
    Opportunities for Retirees to Volunteer 141
    Community Involvement Benefits 143
    Discovering Valuable Methods for Participation 144

Chapter 20 146
A Guide to Preparing for Retirement 146

Chapter 21 151
Important Questions for Baby Boomers Approaching Retirement 151
    Evaluating Preparedness for Finances 151
    Assessing Long-Term Care Programs 152

Conclusion 155

Accepting the Transition into Retirement ..155

Introduction

Overview of Digital Age Retirement

Retirement's Development in the Digital Age
Retirement has changed significantly in recent years; it was once thought of as a time to unwind after a lifetime of hard

labor. Retirement planning and living have changed as a result of the digital era's rapid technical breakthroughs and pervasive internet access. This chapter examines how retirement has changed in the digital age, stressing the value of keeping up with the latest developments and laying out the objectives of this book.

Retirement used to be commonly associated with a passive stage of life that began with the end of work and the start of a period of leisure. Social Security, pensions, and savings were the main sources of income for many retirees. However, a number of factors, such as longer life expectancies, shifting economic conditions, and the introduction of digital technologies, have significantly altered the retirement environment.

Extended Life Expectancy

An extended life expectancy is one of the most important elements impacting the evolution of retirement. People are living longer, healthier lives as a result of improvements in living conditions and healthcare. This is definitely a good thing, but it also means that retirees will have to budget for longer periods of time without receiving income from a typical job. The possibility of retiring at the age of 20, 30, or even longer calls for careful budgeting and thought about how to continue leading an active and satisfying life.

Financial Situation

The state of the economy has a significant impact on retirement. Retirement savings and investment returns have been impacted recently by shifting interest rates, inflation, and market volatility. Additionally, a large portion of the duty for financial planning has shifted from employers to employees with the transition from defined-benefit pension plans to defined-contribution plans like 401(k)s. As a result of this shift, people must now manage their retirement assets more proactively and decide on their financial destiny with knowledge.

Technological Progress

Digital technology's growth is arguably the most significant influence on retirement in the modern world. The way individuals connect with each other, manage their finances, and obtain information has changed dramatically as a result of the widespread use of cellphones, the internet, and other digital technologies. Technology presents retirees with previously unheard-of possibilities to improve their retirement in a number of significant ways:

Financial Management: Retirees have simple access to their financial accounts thanks to digital tools and online platforms, which enable them to keep an eye on investments, keep tabs on spending, and create and modify budgets in real time.

Retirement fund management is made simpler for seniors by automated investing techniques and tailored guidance provided by robo-advisors and financial planning applications.

Healthcare receive: Retirees may manage chronic diseases, interact with medical professionals, and receive medical information from the comfort of their homes thanks to telemedicine and health-monitoring applications. Those who live in rural locations or have mobility challenges would especially benefit from this ease.

Social Connectivity: By keeping seniors in touch with friends and family using social media platforms, video conferencing, and messaging apps, retirees might have less emotions of loneliness and isolation. Online communities and interest groups offer avenues for social connection and involvement, thereby cultivating a feeling of purpose and belonging.

Lifelong Learning: There are a plethora of educational materials available on the internet, ranging from webinars and online courses to virtual libraries and museums. Retirement promotes cognitive health and personal fulfillment because it allows retirees to take up new hobbies, learn new skills, and engage in intellectual stimulation.

The Value of Remaining Up to Date on Current Trends

Retirement planning requires retirees to stay up to date on the latest developments in the ever changing digital world. People may make educated judgments and adjust to new possibilities and challenges by being aware of social, technological, and economic advances. Remaining informed is essential for a successful retirement for the following reasons:

Monetary stability

Retirement savings and investment returns are directly impacted by economic trends such as market performance, inflation rates, and interest rates. Retirees who stay up to date on these issues are better able to make strategic financial decisions regarding when and how to take withdrawals, modify investment portfolios, and maximize Social Security payments. Retirees can also reduce their tax obligations and optimize their retirement income by being aware of changes in tax rules and regulations.

Benefits of Technology

Retirees who stay up to date on technology developments can use digital tools and services to improve their quality of life. For instance, health management, financial security, and social connectivity can all be enhanced by modern health-monitoring gadgets, financial planning applications, and communication platforms. Retirees who are open to embracing new technologies can also maintain their independence and community involvement.

Well-being and Health

Maintaining physical and mental well-being in retirement

Requires being up to date on health trends and advances in medicine. This include being aware of wellness habits, innovative treatment choices, and preventive care strategies. Retirees who are knowledgeable about insurance and healthcare policies are guaranteed to have access to the tools and assistance they need to properly manage their health.

Social Interaction

Retirees can better traverse the shifting terrain of retirement lives by being aware of social and demographic changes. This involves being informed of social events, volunteer opportunities, and community living choices that can enhance their retirement. Having a sense of purpose and being happy in general are influenced by maintaining relationships with others and engaging in worthwhile activities.

Lifetime Education

There are countless chances for lifelong learning in the digital era. Retirees can continue to develop and discover new interests by keeping up with educational resources, cultural events, and intellectual activities. Lifelong learning has been shown to improve mental health, increase self-worth, and give a feeling of accomplishment.

Objectives of the Guide

This guide's main objective is to assist those who intend to retire in 2024 in navigating the prospects and complexities of contemporary retirement. This guide intends to empower retirees to make informed decisions and achieve a secure and joyful retirement by offering insights, trends, and helpful recommendations. The primary aims of this handbook are delineated in the following objectives:

A thorough comprehension of retirement trends

The goal of this guide is to give readers a comprehensive overview of the state of retirement today, covering social, technical, and economic issues. Readers will obtain important insights into the ways in which different elements impact retirement planning and decision-making by closely examining these trends.

Adequate Techniques for Financial Planning

One essential element of a prosperous retirement is financial stability. This book provides doable tactics for handling investments, retirement savings, and spending. The knowledge that follows will help readers plan for long-term financial stability, manage market volatility, and maximize their financial resources.

Accepting Technology

Technology is essential to modern retirement living. The advantages of digital tools and services, such as telemedicine platforms and financial management apps, are highlighted in this handbook. The ability to use technology to stay connected, enhance quality of life, and obtain necessary resources will be imparted to readers.

Advice on Health and Wellbeing

Remaining healthy is essential to having a happy retirement. Information on wellness habits, preventive care, and healthcare options is included in this resource. The skills of good health management, obtaining medical care, and long-term care planning will be imparted to readers.

Engagement in the Social and Community

Retirement-related emotional well-being depends on social networks and community involvement. This manual provides guidance on creating and managing social networks, looking into volunteer opportunities, and getting involved in the community. The strategies to remain engaged, meaningful, and active will be shown to readers.

Lifelong Learning and Individual Development

Retirement offers the chance to pursue lifelong learning and personal growth. This handbook encourages retirees to take up new hobbies, learn new skills, and read for pleasure. The materials and suggestions for lifelong learning will benefit readers' mental well-being and sense of fulfillment.

Resolving Typical Retirement Fears

Retirement may bring with it feelings of unease and uncertainty. Common retirement anxieties like health problems, social isolation, and financial instability are covered in this guide. Readers will feel more confident and equipped to handle the challenges of retirement by offering helpful advice and workable answers.

Establishing a Helpful Environment

A happy retirement requires a supporting atmosphere. This article examines a number of living situations, such as aging in place and retirement communities. The skills necessary to design a secure, cozy, and interesting home that suits their tastes and requirements will be imparted to readers.

Retirement in the digital era brings with it special possibilities as well as difficulties. A proactive and knowledgeable approach is necessary given the ways that retirement has evolved due to factors including longer life expectancies, improved economic situations, and technological improvements. Keeping up with the latest developments is essential for making educated choices and adjusting to changing circumstances. The purpose of this guide is to arm retirees with the information, tactics, and tools necessary to successfully negotiate the challenges of contemporary retirement living. Retirees can have a happy, safe, and active retirement by embracing the digital age and remaining informed.

We'll go into more detail about the major themes and approaches to retirement in 2024 in the upcoming chapters, providing you with professional analysis and helpful tips to help you prepare for and enjoy your golden years. This guide intends to be a helpful tool on your path to a happy and productive retirement, regardless of where you are in the process of making retirement plans.

Chapter 1
Retirement-Related Economic Trends

The preparation and results of retirement are greatly impacted by economic developments in today's globally integrated and dynamic globe. Developing a solid retirement plan requires an understanding of the effects of market volatility, inflation, interest rates, and worldwide economic trends. This chapter explores these economic aspects and emphasizes how crucial it is to make thoughtful financial plans in order to guarantee stability and security of funds in retirement.

Interest rates and inflation's effects

The Silent Erosion of Purchasing Power: Inflation

Over time, inflation, or the general rate of increase in the prices of goods and services, reduces one's purchasing power. This implies that in the future, retirees will be able to purchase less products and services with the same amount of money. Understanding and planning for inflation is vital since even mild inflation can severely impair long-term retirement savings and income.

Inflation: The Silent Erosion of Purchasing Power

Over time, inflation, or the general rate of increase in the prices of goods and services, reduces one's purchasing power. This implies that in the future, retirees will be able to purchase less products and services with the same amount of money. Because even mild inflation can have a major impact on long-term retirement savings and income, it is imperative to understand inflation and make plans for it.

Historical Angle

Inflation rates have fluctuated greatly throughout history due to a variety of external variables, including geopolitical events, market dynamics, and economic policy. For example, there was a lot of inflation throughout the 1970s and early 1980s, with annual rates occasionally rising beyond 10%. Inflation has been very low recently, frequently averaging between two and three percent per year. Nonetheless, over the course of a 20–30 year retirement term, even an apparently low inflation rate can dramatically reduce purchasing power.

Present Patterns and Forecasts

As of 2024, supply chain interruptions, changing energy prices, and the post-pandemic economic recovery have all had an impact on inflation rates. Even though monetary policy is the primary tool used by central banks, like the US Federal Reserve, to control inflation, unanticipated inflationary forces can arise from outside sources. In order to modify their financial plans appropriately, retirees need to stay up to date on the latest trends and estimates regarding inflation.

Effect on Income from Retirement

Inflation can cause fixed-income sources, including pensions and some annuities, to lose actual value over time. For instance, if inflation averages 3% yearly in 20 years, a pension that pays $3,000 per month now may have substantially less purchasing power. In order to counteract this, retirees ought to think about income streams and investments that can beat inflation, such real estate, stocks, and inflation-protected securities like **Treasury Inflation-Protected Securities (TIPS).**

Interest rates: How They Affect Investment Returns and the Cost of Borrowing

The cost of borrowing and the yield on savings and investments are impacted by interest rates, which are determined by central banks. Interest rate fluctuations can have a significant effect on retirees, especially those who depend on fixed-income investments.

The current landscape of interest rates

In recent years, there have been notable swings in interest rates. Global central banks reduced interest rates during the

COVID-19 epidemic in an effort to boost economic growth. In order to counteract inflationary pressures, rates started to rise as the economy recovered. When it comes to borrowing and investing, retirees must have a thorough understanding of the present interest rate environment and its trajectory.

Effect on Investments with Fixed Income

Bonds, certificates of deposit (CDs), and savings accounts are examples of fixed-income investments whose income can be negatively impacted by low interest rates. Low rates might put a hardship on retirees whose income comes from these investments. On the other hand, increasing interest rates may boost returns on fresh fixed-income investments while depressing the bond market value.

Effect on the Cost of Borrowing

For retirees thinking about home equity loans, mortgages, or other forms of credit, interest rates also have an impact on the cost of borrowing. Borrowing becomes more affordable with lower rates, which is advantageous for people trying to finance big purchases or pay off debt. Rising rates do, however, result in higher borrowing costs, which can affect cash flow and financial planning as a whole.

Market volatility and global economic trends' effects

Global Economic Trends: A World Linked and Complicated

More than ever, the world economy is interconnected, and developments in one area can have a significant impact on the entire planet. Comprehending these worldwide patterns is crucial for retirees to manage risks and make well-informed investing decisions.

Cycles of Economic Growth and Recession

Natural economic cycles of expansion and contraction can have an effect on retirement portfolios. Economic expansion periods are typically associated with greater investment returns, whereas recessions may cause market declines and a decline in the value of assets. Retirees can better predict and manage economic cycles by keeping up with global economic indices like GDP growth, unemployment rates, and consumer confidence.

Events in Geopolitics

Market volatility and economic uncertainty can result from geopolitical events like trade wars, conflicts, and political unrest. Trade conflicts, for example, can cause supply chain disruptions, impact business profitability, and result in market sell-offs between major economies. It is imperative for retirees to stay abreast of global changes and contemplate the potential effects on their investments.

Technological Progress

Automation, AI, and renewable energy are examples of technological innovations that are changing economies and industries. These developments upend established industries while also opening up new investment opportunities. It is advisable for retirees to contemplate expanding their investment portfolios by incorporating exposure to burgeoning businesses and emerging technology.

Managing Market Volatility: Managing Ups and Downs

The frequency and magnitude of price swings in financial markets are referred to as market volatility. While some degree of volatility is normal, large swings can affect investment returns and cause worry.

Market Volatility's Sources

Numerous factors, such as the release of economic data, business earnings reports, geopolitical events, and shifts in investor attitude, can cause market volatility. Retirees can avoid making rash judgments and maintain composure during market instability by understanding the causes of volatility.

Effect on Retirement Portfolios

Retirement portfolios are susceptible to various impacts from volatile markets. Significant price fluctuations in equity investments could have an effect on the total value of retirement savings. Even though they are typically more stable, fixed-income investments are nonetheless subject to credit risk and variations in interest rates. Retirees should evaluate their investment horizon and risk tolerance in order to choose an asset allocation that strikes a balance between stability and growth potential.

Techniques for Handling Unpredictability

Pensioners can use a variety of tactics to control market volatility, including:

Diversification is the process of distributing investments among a variety of industries, geographical areas, and asset classes in order to lower risk and stabilize returns. Having a diverse portfolio makes it more likely that strong results in one area will balance out weaker results in another.

Rebalancing: Maintaining the intended asset allocation in the portfolio through regular rebalancing can assist control risk. Rebalancing is the process of purchasing underperforming assets and selling well-performing ones in order to keep the portfolio in line with the retiree's risk tolerance and goals.

Income-Producing Assets: In times of market volatility, holding income-producing assets, such as bonds and stocks that pay dividends, can provide a consistent flow of income.

During recessions, this revenue can lessen the need to liquidate assets in order to pay bills.

Long-Term View: Keeping an eye on the big picture is essential when the market is volatile. Retirees should steer clear of making snap decisions based on market swings and instead concentrate on their long-term financial objectives.

Strategic Financial Planning's Significance

Navigating the economic trends that impact retirement requires strategic financial planning. Retirees can retain their preferred lifestyle, secure their financial future, and deal with unforeseen obstacles with the support of a well-thought-out plan.

Entire Financial Evaluation

A thorough evaluation of the retiree's financial status forms the basis of strategic financial planning. This assessment looks at sources of income, expenses, liabilities, assets, and future financial needs. Important elements of a financial evaluation consist of:

Net Worth Calculation: Deducting liabilities from assets is the first step in calculating net worth. Knowing one's net worth gives one an overview of one's total financial situation and can be used to pinpoint areas that need improvement.

Income Analysis: To ascertain whether retirement income is adequate, it is essential to evaluate both existing and anticipated income sources, including Social Security, pensions, investments, and part-time work.

Expense Analysis: Retirees can better understand their cash flow requirements by assessing their existing and projected expenses. Essential costs, discretionary spending, and prospective medical expenses should all be taken into consideration in this study.

Establishing Goals

A crucial component of strategic financial planning is establishing specific financial objectives. Set goals to help retirees prioritize their financial decisions by giving them focus and direction. Typical retirement objectives consist of:

Income Replacement: Calculating the required income in retirement to sustain the desired standard of living.

Emergency Fund: Setting up an emergency fund to protect finances and pay for unforeseen costs.

Debt reduction: Creating a strategy to pay off debt in order to lessen retirement financial strains.

Estate Planning: Drafting an estate plan helps to avoid potential estate taxes and guarantees that assets are dispersed in accordance with the retiree's desires.

Long-Term Care and Healthcare Expenses: Make plans for these costs in order to guard against major financial hazards.

Investment Plan

A successful investing plan fits the retiree's time horizon, risk tolerance, and financial objectives. Important components of a plan for investing comprise:

Asset Allocation: Determining the right combination of asset types, such as stocks, fixed income, and real estate, to balance risk and return is known as asset allocation.

Spreading investments throughout several markets, industries, and geographical areas in order to lower risk is known as diversification.

Risk management: Applying strategies to control market volatility and preserve the intended asset allocation, such as rebalancing.

Income Generation: Including investments that generate dividends, such stocks and bonds, in order to create a consistent flow of income.

Tax Efficiency: Taking into consideration investment techniques that minimize capital gains taxes and make use of tax-advantaged accounts (such as IRAs and 401(k)s).

Periodic Evaluation and Modification

The process of financial planning is dynamic and ongoing, requiring constant observation and modification. In the face of shifting conditions, the retiree's financial plan should continue to be applicable and successful if they continue to be proactive and flexible.

Annual evaluations: Maintaining retirement goals requires conducting annual evaluations. Amidst these evaluations, retirees ought to:

Evaluate Progress: Determine if the financial objectives are being fulfilled and, if not, make the required modifications.

Examine assets: To preserve the intended asset allocation, evaluate the performance of the assets and think about rebalancing the portfolio.

Update Assumptions: Make that your assumptions about market returns, interest rates, and inflation are still reasonable and consistent with the current environment.

Modify your spending plans: Adjust budgets to reflect current spending and projected needs.

Life Events

Important life events can have an effect on financial goals, requiring revisions and alterations. Retirees ought to think about the following:

Retirement Transition: A different approach is needed when moving from accumulation to distribution. Make sure your sources of income and your spending match, and that your withdrawal rates are manageable.

Health Changes: Medical costs may rise as a result of health problems. Make the necessary updates to long-term care and healthcare plans.

Family Changes: Things like getting married, getting divorced, having grandchildren, or losing a spouse can have an impact on financial goals. Examine and modify agreements to provide financial support, beneficiaries, and estate plans.

Market and Economic Developments: Keep abreast with developments in the markets and economy. Modify investment plans to take advantage of opportunities and reduce risks.

Strategic Financial Planning's Significance
Hazard Assessment

A key element of strategic financial planning is efficient risk management. A retiree's financial security may be affected by a number of hazards, such as longevity risk, inflation risk, market risk, and healthcare expenditures. These risks can be reduced with the use of risk management techniques.

Risk to the Market

The possibility of investment losses as a result of market changes is referred to as market risk. It is advisable for retirees to:

Diversify Investments: Invest in a variety of asset classes, industries, and geographical areas to spread your risk across a wider range of markets.

Asset Allocation: Depending on your time horizon and risk tolerance, keep a suitable mix of fixed income, stocks, and other assets.

Rebalancing: To preserve the intended asset allocation and control risk, rebalance the portfolio periodically.

Risk of Longevity

The risk of outliving one's savings is known as longevity risk. This risk becomes more important for retirees as life expectancies rise. Among the methods to reduce the risk of longevity are:

Annuities: Take into consideration annuities that offer lifetime income guarantees. This can assist guarantee a consistent flow of money for the duration of one's life.

Maintainable Rates of Withdrawal: Create a withdrawal plan that strikes a balance between the requirement for income and principal preservation. Typical recommendations call for withdrawing no more than 4% of the portfolio each year.

Risk of Inflation

Over time, inflation reduces purchasing power, so for retirees, it is a major problem. To control the risk of inflation, think about:

Invest in assets that typically keep up with or exceed inflation, such as real estate, TIPS, and stocks. These are known as inflation-protected investments.

Adjustments for Cost of Living: To help preserve purchasing power, select pension and annuity options that incorporate cost of living adjustments (COLAs).

Medical Expenses

In retirement, healthcare costs can be significant and erratic. Among the methods to control healthcare expenses are:

Health Savings Accounts (HSAs): Establish a tax-advantaged fund for future medical bills by contributing to HSAs during your working years.

Medicare and Supplemental Insurance: Recognize your alternatives for Medicare coverage, and if there are any coverage gaps, think about getting supplemental insurance.

Examine whether you require long-term care insurance to assist with paying for the expenses of in-home care services that Medicare does not cover.

Tax Guidance

Careful tax preparation can protect wealth and increase retirement income. For retirees, the best way to reduce taxes and increase their after-tax income is to think about tax-efficient solutions.

Advantageous Tax Accounts

To reduce tax obligations, make use of tax-advantaged retirement funds, such as IRAs, 401(k)s, and Roth IRAs:

Conventional IRAs and 401(k)s: You pay ordinary income tax on withdrawals, and your contributions are tax deductible. These accounts are advantageous when income is high and tax deductions are significant.

Roth IRAs: Tax-free withdrawals are available, but contributions are made using after-tax money. For people who anticipate retiring in a higher tax bracket, Roth IRAs are a good option.

Tax-Motivated Retractions

Create a withdrawal plan to cut down on taxes:

Roth Conversions: Converting assets from a regular IRA or 401(k) to a Roth IRA is something to think about, especially in years when your taxable income is lower. This can generate income that is tax-free and lower future tax obligations.

Strategic Withdrawals: The goal of strategic withdrawals is to develop tax-deferred accounts by taking withdrawals from taxable accounts first. Think about how Social Security benefits and required minimum distributions (RMDs) may affect your taxes.

Management of Capital Gains
Control capital gains to reduce tax liability

Tax-Loss Harvesting: Sell underperforming investments to offset capital gains against losses.

Advantages of Long-Term vs. Short-Term Capital Gains:

Long-term capital gains have a lower tax rate than short-term gains.

Strategic Financial Planning's Significance
Estate & Legacy Planning

Strategic financial planning must include legacy and estate planning in order to guarantee that beneficiaries are taken care of and that assets are dispersed in accordance with the retiree's desires.

Fundamentals of Estate Planning

Making legal agreements that specify how assets will be handled and allocated after death is known as estate planning. Important components consist of:

Wills: A will appoints an executor to oversee the estate and outlines the distribution of assets. It also permits minor children's guardians to be appointed.

Trusts: Trusts can save estate taxes, eliminate the need for probate, and offer more control over the transfer of assets.

Irrevocable trusts, special needs trusts, and revocable living trusts are common varieties.

Beneficiary Designations: Verify that beneficiary choices are current and consistent with the entire estate plan on retirement accounts, life insurance policies, and other assets.

Advanced Techniques for Planning

Complex estates can benefit from advanced planning techniques that reduce taxes and safeguard assets:

Charitable Giving: To lower inheritance taxes and further charitable objectives, including charitable contributions in the estate plan. Donor-advised funds and charitable remainder trusts are among the available options.

Giving: Use the yearly exclusions from gift taxes to give assets to heirs while you are still living. In addition to lowering the taxable estate, this can give beneficiaries cash support.

Life Insurance: Use life insurance to distribute inheritances among heirs equally or to offer liquidity for estate taxes.

Retirement planning is greatly impacted by economic trends, such as interest rates, inflation, global economic changes, and market volatility. Retirees can protect their financial future by making educated decisions by being aware of these developments and their ramifications.

Having a strategic financial strategy is crucial to overcoming the challenges of retirement. Regular financial assessments, goal-setting, the creation of investment strategies, risk management, tax planning, and legacy planning are all components of a holistic strategy. Retirees can attain their financial objectives and preserve financial stability throughout retirement by remaining proactive and flexible.

In the end, careful preparation for retirement necessitates a blend of intelligence, alertness, and adaptability. Retirees can ensure their financial future and safely handle the challenges of retirement by keeping up with economic changes and making regular adjustments to their financial plans.

Chapter 2

Retirement Planning with Technological Advancements

Retirement planning has undergone a transformation in the digital age due to developments in technology. Technology has completely changed how seniors handle their finances, get healthcare, and maintain relationships with their loved ones. From complex internet platforms to intuitive mobile apps, technology has changed all of these things. This chapter offers insights into the digital tools available to retirees and examines how technology might improve the retirement experience.

Digital Resources for Money Management

The availability of digital tools for financial management is one of the biggest advantages of technology improvements in retirement planning. With the help of these tools, retirees may better than ever manage their money, keep an eye on their investments, and make plans for future needs. Among the most important digital tools for money management are:

Applications for budgeting: With budgeting applications, retirees may keep tabs on their earnings and outlays, establish financial objectives, and follow their spending patterns in real time. Well-known budgeting applications like PocketGuard, YNAB (You Need a Budget), and Mint give users information about their financial situation and assist them in making wise financial decisions.

Investment Platforms: Retirees can easily manage their investment portfolios from their desktops or mobile devices with the help of online investment platforms. Retirees can diversify their portfolios and maximize their investment returns by using these platforms, which provide access to a large array of investment options, such as equities, bonds, mutual funds, and ETFs (Exchange-Traded Funds).

Retirement Calculators: Retirees can use retirement calculators to predict their future income requirements, evaluate their readiness for retirement, and see if they are on track to reach their financial objectives. To generate personalized retirement forecasts, these calculators take into account variables including Social Security payouts, savings, investment returns, retirement age, and life expectancy.

Tax Planning Software: For retirees, tax planning software streamlines the preparation and filing of taxes. By automating tax computations, locating credits and deductions, and producing accurate tax forms, these software solutions minimize error risk and increase tax savings.

Mobile Apps and Web Sites for seniors

Apart from financial management tools, retirees' wants and preferences are specifically catered to through online platforms and mobile apps. These platforms include a plethora of features and services aimed at augmenting retirement enjoyment and enhancing general well-being. Retirement-focused websites and mobile applications include, for instance:

Healthcare applications: Retirees may easily access medical services, information, and resources with the help of healthcare applications. These apps encourage proactive healthcare management and better health outcomes by enabling users to make appointments, renew medicines, track health data, and connect with medical professionals remotely.

Social networking sites: Retiree-specific social networking sites promote leisure activities, community involvement, and social bonds. With the help of these platforms, retirees can fight social isolation and loneliness by meeting like-minded people, joining interest-based groups, taking part in online events, and sharing experiences and memories with friends and family.

Learning Platforms: Retirees can enhance their skills, pursue personal growth, and continue their education using learning platforms. With the abundance of courses, tutorials, and resources available on these platforms, retirees can keep intellectually active in retirement by pursuing new interests and hobbies.

Apps for travel and leisure: Apps for travel and leisure serve retirees' interests in discovering new places, organizing trips, and engaging in leisure activities. Retirees may easily plan memorable excursions and experiences with the help of these apps, which offer information on travel destinations, lodging alternatives, transit options, and local attractions.

Improving the Retirement Experience with Technology

All things considered, technology has completely changed what it means to be a retiree, providing them with never-before-seen levels of accessibility, ease, and power. Through the use of digital tools, smartphone apps, and websites, retirees can:

Take Charge of Finances: Track spending, manage funds more effectively, and choose wisely when making investments.

Access Healthcare Services: From the convenience of their homes, patients can simply make appointments, get in touch with medical professionals, and keep an eye on key health indicators.

Stay Connected: To lessen feelings of loneliness and isolation, cultivate social connections, participate in groups, and uphold relationships with friends and family.

Follow Your Interests: In order to foster personal development and contentment in retirement, keep learning, take up new hobbies, and engage in leisure activities.

Furthermore, technology has democratized access to healthcare and financial planning services, lowering costs and increasing accessibility for retirees from all socioeconomic backgrounds. The user-friendly nature of contemporary technology guarantees that everyone can profit from its revolutionary potential in retirement planning, regardless of how tech-savvy or inexperienced retirees are with digital tools.

To sum up, technology has completely changed the retirement planning process by providing retirees with a plethora of digital tools, mobile applications, and web platforms to help them manage their money, get access to healthcare, and improve their general well-being. Retirees can confidently and conveniently pursue their particular hobbies and passions, stay in touch with loved ones, and take charge of their financial destinies by utilizing technology. The retirement experience will surely become even more individualized, empowering, and gratifying for retirees worldwide as technology advances

Chapter 3

Planning for Retirement Amidst Social and Demographic Changes

Traditional ideas about what it means to retire have been challenged by societal and demographic changes that have changed the retirement planning landscape in recent years. The rise of non-traditional retirement lives can be attributed to various factors, including heightened life expectancy, shifting perspectives on work and leisure, and changing lifestyle preferences. This chapter offers insights into alternate retirement possibilities while examining the effects of these social and demographic changes on seniors.

Extended Life Expectancy and Its Consequences

The longer life expectancy is one of the biggest social and demographic changes affecting retirement planning. People are living longer thanks to improvements in lifestyle, diet, and healthcare. Many people are now well into their 80s and 90s and beyond. Even while longer life expectancies are unquestionably a good thing, retirees face particular difficulties and things to take into account:

Extended Retirement time: Due to longer life expectancies, retirees may need to finance a longer retirement time. To make sure that funds continue during retirement, prudent asset management and financial planning are necessary.

Healthcare expenses: As retirees may need medical care and support services for longer periods of time, longer lifespans translate into higher healthcare expenses. It's critical to make plans for long-term care and medical costs in order to prevent financial hardship in retirement.

Social and Emotional Well-Being: Longer retirement periods give retirees chances for meaningful experiences, personal development, and fulfillment. But as one ages, sustaining social ties, engaging in hobbies, and keeping one's mind active become even more important for enhancing general wellbeing and quality of life.

Intergenerational Relationships: Retirees may have more time to spend with younger generations, such as children, grandchildren, and great-grandchildren, as a result of living longer. Retirees' lives can be improved and given a sense of purpose and connection by fostering and developing relationships across generations.

Unconventional Retirement Ways of Living

A growing number of retirees are choosing unconventional retirement lifestyles that stray from accepted conventions in reaction to shifting social and demographic trends. These other retirement options provide more independence, flexibility, and chances for personal growth. Non-traditional retirement lifestyles include, for instance:

Community Living: Retirees can live with like-minded people, share resources, and take part in group activities in retirement communities, co-housing arrangements, and intentional communities. These living situations provide retirees with social support, company, and a feeling of community, creating a lively and encouraging atmosphere.

Part-Time Work: Many retirees opt to move into part-time or flexible work arrangements instead of completely leaving the workforce. In addition to giving retirees the chance to pursue personal interests, give back to the community, and preserve their sense of purpose and identity, part-time work enables them to remain financially comfortable, active, and involved.

Continuing Education: Retirees looking for intellectual stimulation and growth are beginning to place a greater emphasis on lifelong learning and personal development. Retirees can enrich their retirement experience and improve their cognitive health by participating in lifetime learning activities and exploring new topics and skills through adult learning centers, online courses, and continuing education programs.

Volunteerism and Civic Engagement: Volunteering and civic engagement are popular among retirees because they allow them to stay involved in society, give back to their communities, and have a beneficial influence. There are many options for retirees to volunteer their time, skills, and knowledge to worthwhile causes in fields like social services, healthcare, education, and environmental conservation.

Accepting Non-Traditional Retirement Ways of Living

Adopting a non-traditional retirement lifestyle necessitates meticulous planning and preparation in addition to a mental adjustment. When contemplating alternate retirement possibilities, retirees ought to:

Consider Your Personal Values and Retirement objectives

Give your retirement objectives, interests, and values some thought. Prioritize in your retirement planning the things that make life happy, fulfilled, and meaningful—experiences, relationships, and activities.

Investigate and Explore Communities, Resources, and Opportunities

Look into and investigate communities, resources, and non-traditional retirement living, employment, education, and participation opportunities. Take into account elements including pricing, location, amenities, and suitability for your goals and lifestyle.

Formulate a Complete Retirement Strategy: Formulate a complete retirement strategy that takes into account lifestyle factors, healthcare planning, financial preparation, and social and mental health. Seek expert advice and assistance as necessary to make sure that the retirement plan is in line with your objectives and values.

Remain Adaptable and Open-Minded: As situations change and develop, be willing to adjust plans and consider new options. Navigating the ambiguities and difficulties of retirement and appreciating the diversity and complexity of non-traditional retirement lifestyles require flexibility and an open mind.

Retirement planning has been reinterpreted in light of social and demographic changes, which have opened the door for less conventional retirement lives that provide more flexibility, independence, and chances for personal fulfillment. Alternative retirement choices like communal living, part-time job, continuing education, and volunteerism have become more popular due to factors like longer life expectancies, shifting attitudes about work and leisure, and changing lifestyle preferences.

Retirees can design meaningful and happy retirement experiences by embracing non-traditional retirement lifestyles and giving own beliefs, interests, and aspirations first priority. Retirement communities, part-time employment, and lifelong learning are just a few of the many options available to retirees to learn, grow, and improve society while also improving their own and others' quality of life.

Chapter 4

In 2024, where would be the best place to retire?

Selecting the best place to retire is an important choice that will affect your total retirement experience, financial security, and quality of life. Retirement travelers have an abundance of possibilities to choose from in 2024, from well-liked U.S. states with amenities geared toward seniors to up-and-coming foreign locations with desirable lifestyles at significantly lower costs. The greatest places to retire in 2024 are examined in this chapter, taking into consideration a number of variables like cost of living, taxation, access to healthcare, climate, and community.

Top Retirement States in the United States

Florida: Well-known for its pleasant weather, multicultural neighborhoods, and wealth of leisure opportunities, Florida continues to be a popular destination for retirees. The state is home to many retirement-friendly towns and cities, like as Sarasota, Naples, and St. Petersburg, which provide good healthcare, cheap taxes, and reasonably priced housing options.

North Carolina: Due to its stunning scenery, lively culture, and reasonably priced cost of living, North Carolina is becoming a more popular destination for retirees looking for a laid-back but busy lifestyle. Retirees find cities like Asheville, Chapel Hill, and Charlotte to be attractive because they combine natural beauty with urban conveniences.

South Carolina: Many people find South Carolina to be a desirable retirement destination due to its pleasant temperature, historic cities, and quaint seaside villages. Places with a relaxed vibe, cultural attractions, and excellent access to healthcare are Charleston, Hilton Head Island, and Greenville.

Arizona: Well-known for its breathtaking desert vistas, abundant outdoor leisure options, and reasonably priced housing, Arizona is a well-liked option for retirees looking for a warm environment and a busy way of life. For retirees, cities like Phoenix, Tucson, and Scottsdale provide lots of sunshine, affordable housing, and a choice of housing options.

Texas: With its burgeoning economy, varied culture, and reasonably priced cost of living, Texas is becoming a more and more well-liked retirement destination. A variety of amenities are available in cities like Austin, San Antonio, and Houston, including first-rate medical facilities, interesting cultural attractions, and leisure pursuits.

New International Retirement Resorts

Mexico: Many Americans find Mexico to be a desirable retirement destination due to its close proximity to the United States, affordable cost of living, and pleasant environment. Well-known expat settlements with a rich cultural history, a laid-back lifestyle, and reasonably priced healthcare alternatives include Puerto Vallarta, San Miguel de Allende, and Merida.

Portugal: For seniors seeking to live a European lifestyle without going over budget, Portugal's picturesque coastline, historic cities, and advantageous tax laws make it a desirable choice. A thriving expat community, first-rate healthcare facilities, and a high standard of living can be found in places like Lisbon, Porto, and the Algarve region.

Costa Rica: For retirees looking for a tranquil but exciting retirement, Costa Rica is a popular choice due to its natural beauty, eco-friendly culture, and reasonably priced living. Cities with tropical temperatures, a laid-back culture, and easy access to top-notch medical facilities are San Jose, Escazu, and Tamarindo.

Panama: Many foreigners find Panama to be a suitable retirement location due to its contemporary infrastructure, tax incentives, and stable economy. A wide range of amenities are available in cities like Panama City, Boquete, and Bocas del

Toro, including reasonably priced healthcare, outdoor recreational opportunities, and a friendly expat community.

Things to Take Into Account

It's important to take a number of aspects into account when assessing possible retirement locations to make sure that the area you choose will meet your needs for healthcare, finances, and lifestyle. Among the important things to think about are:

Cost of Living: To ascertain whether the location is within your retirement budget, consider the total cost of living, which includes housing, utilities, groceries, and medical costs.

Tax-Friendliness: To ascertain the financial ramifications of retiring in a specific area, investigate the local tax laws and regulations, including income taxes, property taxes, and sales taxes.

Healthcare Facilities: To be sure you'll have access to the services and medical treatment you require in retirement, evaluate the accessibility and quality of healthcare facilities, including clinics, hospitals, and specialists.

Environment: To decide whether you'll be comfortable living in the location year-round, take into account the destination's environment and weather patterns, including temperature extremes, humidity levels, and seasonal variations.

Community: To make sure you'll be able to live a happy and active retirement lifestyle, investigate the local community and social facilities, such as recreational options, cultural events, and networking and socializing chances.

A number of aspects need to be carefully considered when deciding where would be the ideal place to retire in 2024: cost of living, taxation, access to healthcare, climate, and community. Whether your preference is to retire in a well-liked U.S. state with amenities for retirees or to investigate new international locations that provide appealing lifestyles at a much lower cost, careful planning and research are necessary to guarantee a happy and fulfilling retirement. You can identify the ideal retirement location that satisfies your requirements and improves your general well-being in retirement by assessing your priorities, preferences, and financial objectives.

Chapter 5

Which Month in 2024 Is Best for Retirement?

Retirement is a big change in life that needs to be planned for and taken into great consideration, including deciding when is the best time to start saving for retirement. Retirees will have the chance to carefully plan their retirement in 2024 to maximize their financial gain and comfort of mind. The benefits of retiring toward the end of the year are examined in this chapter, with particular attention paid to the advantages for financial planning, benefits accumulation, Social Security implications, and market timing chances.

Benefits of Year-End Retirement for Financial Planning

Retirees who retire at the end of the year can benefit from a number of financial planning advantages that can help them optimize their financial status and maximize their retirement savings:

Maximizing Retirement Contributions: Retirees can optimize their annual retirement contributions by retiring at the end of the year. Retirees can increase their retirement savings and potentially benefit from tax advantages by funding retirement accounts, such as 401(k)s, IRAs, and other tax-advantaged savings vehicles, to the maximum amount permitted.

Matching contributions from the employer: A lot of companies match employee contributions to retirement plans. Retirees can optimize their retirement savings by opting to retire at the end of the year, which guarantees them the entire benefit of any employer-matched funds for that particular year.

Clear Cutoff for Annual Income: Retiring at the end of the year simplifies financial management and tax planning by offering a clear cutoff for annual income. Retirees can improve their financial condition for the next year and better manage their tax liabilities by quitting employment and income sources prior to the start of the next tax year.

Compiling Benefits and Taking Social Security Into Account

Aside from the benefits of financial planning, retiring at the end of the year enables retirees to profit from Social Security considerations and benefit accumulation:

Accrued Vacation and Sick Leave: Retirees can guarantee they have accrued the maximum amount of vacation and sick leave by retiring at the end of the year. Depending on their employer's policy, these benefits may be paid out upon retirement. Having this extra income can help ease the transition to retirement by offering a financial buffer.

Social Security Timing: The date of retirement may have an impact on the amount of payments that retirees who intend to begin receiving Social Security benefits will receive. Some people may be able to attain full retirement age or postpone benefit claims until a later time by retiring later in the year, which would increase their monthly benefit amount.

Tax Repercussions: Depending on retirees' annual income, Social Security benefits may be taxable. Retirees who retire at the end of the year may be able to minimize the amount of their Social Security benefits that are taxable by better managing their income sources and tax obligations.

Timing of the Market and Year-End Bonuses

Additionally, retiring at the end of the year offers chances to time the market and possibly reap financial rewards:

Year-End Bonuses: A lot of businesses provide their staff with year-end bonuses or other financial incentives. Retirees can increase their retirement savings and financial resources by retiring after obtaining these incentives, giving them more security and freedom in their later years.

Trends in the Financial Market: Retiring at the end of the year gives retirees the opportunity to evaluate the year's financial market conditions and make well-informed choices on their investment portfolios. Retirees can improve the timing of withdrawals from retirement funds and modify their investing strategy by assessing market performance and prospective opportunities or hazards.

It is important to carefully weigh the benefits of financial planning, benefits accumulation, Social Security implications, and market timing opportunities when determining the optimum month to retire in 2024. There are many advantages to retiring at the end of the year, such as simplifying tax preparation, maximizing retirement contributions, and benefiting from employer matching contributions. Furthermore, retiring later in the year can enable seniors to maximize Social Security benefits, collect more vacation and sick leave, and obtain year-end bonuses. Retirees can position themselves for a safe and enjoyable retirement in 2024 and beyond by planning their retirement for optimal financial gain.

Chapter 6

How Much Will You Need in 2024 When You Retire?

One of the most important questions to answer when making retirement plans is how much money you'll need to live comfortably in your golden years. When retirees are ready to start this new chapter of their lives in 2024, it's critical to comprehend the financial aspects of retirement planning. This chapter explores the several aspects of retirement savings goals, such as expected healthcare expenditures, inflation, desired retirement age, and lifestyle expectations. Retirees can better prepare for a safe and satisfying retirement in 2024 and beyond by learning how to calculate retirement needs and the value of individualized financial guidance.

Determine Retirement Requirements Using Lifestyle and Expense Data
Assessing your expected spending and lifestyle expectations is the first step towards estimating how much money you'll need in retirement. A retiree's housing costs, medical expenditures, transportation costs, food costs, recreational activities, and any other discretionary spending they plan to

incur in retirement should all be taken into account. Retirees can estimate their annual expenses and pinpoint areas where their spending habits may need to change in order to achieve their retirement goals by creating a thorough budget.

The general rule is 25 times annual expenses

The amount of money you'll need in retirement is a personal decision, but as a general guideline, you should strive for a retirement nest egg that is 25 times your annual expenses. The 4% withdrawal rate hypothesis, which states that retirees can safely withdraw 4% of their retirement assets annually without running out of money during their lifetime, is the foundation of this guideline. To get an approximate idea of how much you'll need to invest for retirement, multiply your projected annual costs by 25.

70–80% of Pre-Retirement Income to Be Replaced

In general, financial advisors advise trying to maintain your quality of life in retirement by replacing 70–80% of your pre-retirement income. This proportion accounts for the possibility that certain expenses—like those associated with transportation and employment—may go down in retirement while other expenses—like those associated with healthcare and leisure activities—may go up. Setting a target for your retirement savings goal can be achieved by assessing your pre-retirement income and computing 70–80% of that amount.

The Value of Tailored Financial Guidance

Retirement planning can be sparked by broad guidelines and rules of thumb, but it's important to remember that every person's situation is unique, and getting individualized financial counsel is crucial during this process. Retirees can establish their retirement goals and priorities, evaluate their particular financial status, and create a personalized retirement plan with the assistance of a certified financial counselor. Financial advisers may assist seniors negotiate the intricacies of retirement planning with confidence and peace of mind by offering insightful advice on investment options, tax planning, estate planning, and retirement savings techniques.

The amount of money you'll need for retirement in 2024 depends on a number of aspects that need to be carefully considered, such as your planned retirement age, projected spending, expected lifestyle, and inflation. While general guidelines like the 70-80% replacement income guideline and the 25-times expenses rule can serve as useful benchmarks, tailored financial guidance is necessary to create a thorough retirement plan that is in line with your unique objectives and situation. Retirees can improve their chances of having a safe and happy retirement in 2024 and beyond by engaging with a professional financial advisor and approaching retirement planning proactively.

Chapter 7

Insurance and Health Care

One of the most important things for people to think about as they enter retirement in 2024 is healthcare and insurance. Retaining physical health and financial stability in retirement requires having access to high-quality healthcare and adequate insurance coverage. An overview of retiree healthcare options, such as Medicare, private insurance, and supplemental plans, is given in this chapter. It also examines ways to reduce health-related financial concerns and the significance of making long-term care plans.

An overview of supplemental plans, private insurance, and Medicare

1. Medicare: Medicare is a government health insurance program that is mostly available to people 65 years of age and older, as well as some younger people with disabilities. It is divided into various sections:

Medicare Part A: Hospital insurance that provides coverage for skilled nursing facility care, hospice care, inpatient hospital stays, and a portion of home health care services.

Medicare Part B: Health insurance that includes preventative services, durable medical equipment, doctor visits, and outpatient care.

Medicare Part C (Medicare Advantage): Medicare Part C, or Medicare Advantage, refers to plans provided by commercial insurance companies that cover Medicare Parts A and B. These plans frequently include extra benefits like prescription medication coverage and dental or eye care.

Medicare Part D: Prescription drug coverage offered by Medicare-approved private insurance providers

2. Private Insurance: Retirees may decide to purchase private health insurance plans to add to their Medicare benefits or to receive extra benefits not covered by the government's standard Medicare program. Plans offered by private insurance companies may have larger networks of providers, provide coverage for procedures not provided by Medicare, and include extra benefits like dental, eye, and hearing care.

3. Plans for Supplemental Insurance: Also referred to as Medigap plans, these plans are intended to bridge Medicare's coverage gaps by paying for deductibles, copayments, and coinsurance, as well as other out-of-pocket expenses. Private insurance companies provide these policies, which can aid retirees in better managing their medical costs.

Making Long-Term Care Plans

A variety of services and supports aimed at assisting people with long-term diseases, impairments, or other problems that impair their capacity to carry out everyday tasks on their own are together referred to as long-term care. Retirees must plan for long-term care in order to guarantee that they will have the resources and assistance they need as they get older. The following are some methods for making long-term care plans:

Long-Term Care Insurance: Retirees may be able to defray the cost of assisted living, home health care, and nursing home care by purchasing long-term care insurance coverage. These policies usually offer coverage for a predetermined time frame and may have restrictions on eligibility and benefits.

Personal Savings and Investments: To help with future long-term care costs, retirees can put money aside in investment portfolios or personal savings accounts. Retirees can make sure they have enough money set aside to take care of their future care requirements by factoring long-term care expenditures into their total retirement plan.

Medicaid: Medicaid is a combined federal-state program that offers low-income and resource-constrained people health coverage, including long-term care services. States have different eligibility standards and services that are covered, but for retirees who deplete their assets and savings, Medicaid can be a vital safety net.

Sustaining Sufficient Insurance Coverage: It's critical to routinely review and update insurance policies to make sure retirees are sufficiently protected against unforeseen medical costs. To make sure they cover their current healthcare needs, retirees should assess their Medicare coverage, supplemental insurance plans, and private insurance policies.

Examining Techniques for Lowering Healthcare expenditures

Retirees can investigate many approaches to lower healthcare expenditures, like using generic prescription drugs, taking part in wellness initiatives, and utilizing insurance-covered preventative care services. Retirees can also look into healthcare facilities and providers to locate affordable solutions without sacrificing quality of treatment.

When it comes to retirement planning and financial stability, healthcare and insurance are essential. Retirees may handle the intricacies of healthcare with assurance and peace of mind by being aware of their alternatives for healthcare, making plans for their long-term care requirements, and putting mechanisms in place to reduce health-related financial concerns. Retirees can take proactive measures to safeguard their health and financial well-being during retirement in 2024 and beyond, whether by investing in long-term care coverage, buying private insurance, or enrolling in Medicare.

Retirement is the start of a new chapter in life, full with possibilities for development, discovery, and satisfaction. This section looks at a variety of methods and advice to assist retirees get the most out of their golden years. The subject of Chapter 9 is remaining engaged and active. It emphasizes the value of hobbies, physical activity, volunteering, lifelong learning, and personal development in sustaining a happy retirement.

Chapter 8
Remaining Involved and Active

Retirement gives retirees the gift of time, allowing them to engage in hobbies, passions, and pursuits they may have put off while they were employed. Maintaining social ties, mental clarity, and general well-being in retirement depends on continuing to be active and involved in addition to the physical benefits.

Exercise and Interests

Frequent Exercise: Keeping up excellent health and vitality in retirement requires regular physical activity. Selecting an exercise program that fits your interests and capabilities can assist enhance cardiovascular health, strength, flexibility, and balance. Examples of such programs include walking, swimming, cycling, yoga, and tai chi.

Following Interests: Retirement provides the ideal setting for engaging in interests and hobbies that make you happy and fulfilled. Engaging in artistic endeavors during retirement, such as cooking, painting, creating, gardening, or playing an instrument, can bring one a sense of accomplishment and purpose.

Possibilities for Volunteering

Giving Back to the Community: In retirement, volunteering is a meaningful way to stay connected to people, have a positive impact on society, and contribute to society. Retirees can find satisfaction in helping others and giving back to their communities by volunteering at a local food bank, environmental organization, animal shelter, hospital, or charity.

Mentoring and Tutoring: By offering their time as mentors, tutors, or educators, retirees can impart their knowledge, abilities, and life experiences to others. Retirees can stay intellectually fulfilled and make a difference in the lives of others by teaching adult education classes, tutoring students, or serving as mentors to young professionals.

Persistent Education and Individual Development

Lifelong Learning: Retirement is a great time to take advantage of chances for lifelong learning and increase one's knowledge and skill set. Retirees can continue to study and develop intellectually during their retirement years by enrolling in online courses, attending conferences and seminars, or taking classes at a nearby community college.

Travel & Exploration: Having retired gives one the opportunity to travel and discover new places, people, and experiences. Retirees can indulge their wanderlust and make lifelong memories with loved ones by traveling the world, taking road vacations, or going on weekend getaways.

A happy and lively retirement lifestyle depends on continuing to be involved and active. Retirees can find meaning and purpose in retirement by staying connected to others, enriching their life, engaging in physical activities, pursuing hobbies, volunteering, and never stopping learning and growing. Retirees can maximize their retirement years and have a happy and meaningful life after work by partaking in new experiences and adventures, contributing back to the community, or being physically and mentally fit.

Chapter 9
Sustaining Financial Well-Being

Sustaining sound financial standing is essential to a happy retirement. Making the shift from a regular paycheck to a fixed income and savings involves careful preparation, strict budgeting, and astute resource management. This chapter explores how to control your spending and create a budget that works, how important it is to review your financial plan on a regular basis, and how to keep your credit score high while handling debt.

Efficient Expense Management and Budgeting
A sound budget is essential for maintaining financial stability in retirement. Retirees can enjoy their retirement stress-free and make sure their money lasts by creating a well-planned budget.

Evaluating Income Sources: Finding every source of income is the first step in developing a retirement budget. This covers income from part-time employment, Social Security benefits, pensions, retirement account withdrawals, annuities, and rental income, among other sources. Determining the entire monthly revenue is helpful in establishing reasonable spending caps.

Expenses should be divided into two categories: necessary and discretionary. Housing, utilities, food, medical care, insurance, and transportation are examples of essential costs. Discretionary costs include gifts, entertainment, travel, eating out, and hobbies. Putting the most important needs first guarantees that the costs are paid for first.

Making a Detailed Budget: Every monthly and yearly spending should be taken into consideration in a detailed budget. Spending tracking tools include spreadsheets and budgeting applications. The objective is to find places where expenditures can be cut and to match income with expenses.

Making Inflation Adjustments: Over time, inflation can reduce the value of money. Retirees should make sure their investments and savings can exceed inflation and anticipate future costs into their budget in order to accommodate for it.

Emergency Fund: It's important to keep an emergency fund up to date. Unexpected costs can put a burden on finances, such as large home repairs or medical issues. As a safety net, an emergency fund should ideally cover six to twelve months' worth of costs.

Monitoring and Modifying: Budgets are dynamic processes. Changes in income, expenses, and financial objectives can be accommodated by routinely examining and modifying the budget. Retirees can stay within their budget by keeping an eye on their spending patterns and taking proactive measures to make any required modifications.

Frequent Evaluations of Financial Plans

To ensure long-term financial stability and adjust to changing circumstances, regular assessments of the financial plan are important.

Annual Reviews: Retirees should evaluate their financial strategy in-depth at least once a year. This entails analyzing changes in income or expenses, recalculating withdrawal rates, and reviewing the performance of investments.

Expert Financial Advice: Speaking with a financial advisor can help you maximize your retirement savings by offering insightful advice and helpful methods. Advisors ensure that retirees' financial plans are current and strong by helping with tax preparation, investment management, estate planning, and other areas.

Changing Investment Strategies: As retirees get older, their tolerance for risk may shift. In order to ensure that investments remain in line with financial objectives and time horizons, regular assessments enable portfolio adjustments to reflect a more conservative or acceptable risk profile.

Tax Efficiency: Changes in tax rules and regulations can have an impact on retirement expenses and income. Tax efficiency techniques, such as when to take money out of tax-deferred accounts, when to convert to a Roth account, and when to take advantage of tax credits and deductions, should be reviewed on a regular basis.

Estate Planning: Putting together an estate is a continuous activity. Retirees' preferences are honored and their assets are transferred in accordance with their plans when wills, trusts, beneficiary designations, and healthcare directives are updated on a regular basis.

Keeping Your Credit Score High and Taking Care of Your Debt

Retaining a sound credit record and skillfully handling debts are essential elements of sound financial planning in retirement.

Comprehending Credit Scores: A high credit score influences interest rates, insurance premiums, and even loan acceptance. It is important for retirees to be aware of the variables that affect credit ratings, including credit utilization, length of credit history, new credit, and mix of credit.

Monitoring Credit Reports: Retirees can prevent identity theft, find and fix mistakes in their credit reports, and stay up to date on their credit status by routinely reviewing their credit reports from the three major credit agencies (Equifax, Experian, and TransUnion).

Paying Your Bills on Time: Keeping your credit score high requires timely bill payments. Bills are paid on time when automatic payments or reminders are set up, preventing late fees and damage to credit scores.

Handling Debt: In retirement, debt management is essential. Credit card balances and other high-interest obligations can swiftly deplete retirement funds. In order to reduce interest rates and monthly payments, retirees should give priority to paying off high-interest debts and think about refinancing or consolidating debt.

Retirees ought to exercise caution while taking on new debt. While some debts—like mortgages—could be affordable, others might put a strain on one's finances. Maintaining financial stability involves assessing if taking on new debt is necessary and affordable.

Using Credit Sensibly: Keeping a high credit score can be achieved by using credit responsibly. It's wise to use credit only for prearranged and budgeted purchases, pay off credit card debt in full each month, and maintain modest credit card balances.

Emergency Credit: Being able to borrow money in an emergency might be reassuring. It should, however, only be employed sparingly and as a last resort in order to prevent taking on needless debt.

Proactive and disciplined money management is necessary to preserve financial stability in retirement. Retirees who manage their expenses and budget well are able to live within their means and have a clear picture of their financial status. Frequent assessments of financial plans aid in strategy optimization and assist react to changes. Sustaining a sound credit score and prudent debt management are essential components of long-term financial security. Retirees who use these tactics can live stress-free and fulfilled retirement years without worrying about money.

Chapter 10
Mental Health and Social Connectivity

A major turning point in life is retirement, which provides the opportunity to pursue new interests, pastimes, and relationships. But there are drawbacks as well, such losing the professional identity, daily structure, and social networks that come with a job. In order to guarantee a happy and active retirement, it becomes imperative to maintain social connectivity and mental health throughout this time. This chapter examines the value of establishing and preserving social bonds, participating in neighborhood activities, and making use of mental health facilities.

Creating and Preserving Social Networks

Emotional and mental health depend on social relationships. They offer the support, purpose, and sense of belonging that are necessary for a happy retirement.

Recognizing the Value of Social Connections: Having strong social connections can benefit one's physical, mental, and overall well-being. According to research, people who have strong social networks typically live longer, report higher levels of happiness and well-being, and have lower rates of depression.

Reestablishing Contact with Friends and Family: Retirement is a chance to reestablish contact with friends and family. More time spent with close ones can improve bonds and offer emotional support. Frequent interaction, whether via in-person meetings, phone conversations, or video chats, aids in the upkeep of these essential relationships.

Creating New Friends: Retiring offers the opportunity to widen one's social network. Retirees can meet new people with similar interests by joining clubs, interest groups, or volunteer organizations. Finding and interacting with people who share your interests can also be facilitated via social media sites and online forums.

Sustaining a Social Schedule: Retirees can maintain their social networks by establishing a consistent schedule. This can include going to get-togethers every week, going to neighborhood functions, or taking part in group activities. In social interactions, consistency offers structure and aids in the maintenance of strong relationships.

Managing Social Challenges: Due to mobility limitations, health problems, or reclusive dispositions, retirees may find it difficult to make new social contacts. It could be necessary to get out of one's comfort zone in order to overcome these obstacles, as well as look for approachable social opportunities and, if necessary, professional assistance.

Taking Part in Community Activities

Participating actively in community events fosters a sense of fulfillment and purpose in addition to improving social connectivity.

Volunteering: Meeting new people, staying active, and giving back to the community may all be accomplished by volunteering. Retirees are free to select causes that are important to them, such as environmental preservation, volunteering with children, or donating to local charity. Volunteering fosters a sense of community connection and accomplishment.

Joining Clubs and Organizations: A lot of towns have clubs and organizations that serve a range of interests, such as sports teams, art societies, literature clubs, and gardening clubs. Regular chances for social interaction and fun activities are offered by these clubs.

Taking Part in Local Events: Retirees can maintain a sense of community by going to local events like concerts, festivals, fairs, and meetings. These gatherings provide an opportunity to meet people, discover new hobbies, and become immersed in the community.

Lifelong Learning: Attending continuing education classes at nearby colleges, universities, or community centers can be a socially and academically interesting experience. Numerous establishments provide retirement-focused courses on everything from technology and fitness to literature and history.

Taking Up a New Interest or Hobby: Retirement is a great opportunity to take up new interests or revive old ones. Taking part in joyful and fulfilling activities, such as hiking, cooking, painting, or photography, can improve mental health and offer social connection chances.

Developing Community Initiatives: Seniors who possess a strong sense of leadership and a strong sense of community might establish programs like community gardens, neighborhood watch programs, or local support groups. These programs create a feeling of community and offer venues for social engagement.

Making the Most of Mental Health Resources

One of the most important aspects of total wellbeing in retirement is mental health. Retirees can find support in using mental health resources to assist them deal with the psychological and emotional demands of this time of life.

Understanding the Significance of Mental Health: Emotional, psychological, and social well-being are all included in mental health. It influences people's thoughts, feelings, and behaviors and is essential for managing stress, interacting with others, and coming to conclusions.

Recognizing Mental Health Issues: Depression, anxiety, loneliness, and stress are among the common mental health issues that retirees face. These may result from significant life transitions, including as leaving the workforce to retire, losing a loved one, experiencing health problems, or experiencing financial difficulties.

Seeking Professional Assistance: Counseling and therapy are two forms of professional mental health assistance that can be very helpful. Licensed counselors, psychologists, and psychiatrists can offer advice on how to handle mental health issues and enhance emotional stability.

Using Online Resources: A plethora of online resources, such as teletherapy, mental health applications, and instructional websites, are accessible for mental health concerns. These tools make it easy to get expert advice and information, particularly for people who might have privacy concerns or mobility challenges.

Joining Support Groups: Support groups offer a secure setting where members can talk about their experiences and get help from others going through comparable struggles. Groups are available via internet resources, community centers, and medical facilities. They provide both practical guidance and emotional assistance.

Taking Care of Oneself: Maintaining mental health requires self-care routines including consistent physical activity, a balanced diet, enough sleep, and mindfulness exercises like yoga and meditation. These techniques enhance mood, lessen stress, and enhance general wellbeing.

Taking Part in Creative treatments: Expressing emotions and improving mental health can be accomplished through creative treatments including writing, music, and art therapy. These treatments give patients a platform for their artistic and self-expression, which is often very healing.

Sustaining a Positive Attitude: Gratitude exercises and positive outlook cultivation have a big impact on mental health. A sense of fulfillment and contentment can be attained by enjoying modest victories, focusing on the positive elements of retirement, and setting realistic goals.

A happy retirement depends on maintaining mental and social well-being. Creating and sustaining social networks improves general wellbeing, lessens feelings of loneliness, and offers emotional support. Participating in community events gives retirees a feeling of purpose and belonging, and using mental health services guarantees that they can deal with emotional and psychological difficulties. Retirees can have a vibrant, meaningful, and healthy retirement by placing a high priority on their mental health, social contacts, and community involvement.

Chapter 11

Getting Rid of Uncertainty Around Money

Retirement is a time of great expectation and change, but it also comes with difficulties and unknowns, especially in terms of one's financial stability. This chapter looks at ways to become financially stable, how important it is to have diversified investments, and how important emergency savings and contingency planning are.

Techniques for Maintaining Financial Stability
Retirement financial stability necessitates thorough planning and a multifaceted strategy. The following are some crucial tactics:

Developing a Comprehensive Retirement Plan: The foundation of financial security is a comprehensive retirement plan. This plan should contain predicted spending, a budget that fits your retirement lifestyle, and an analysis of expected income sources (such Social Security, pensions, and investments). This strategy should be reviewed and updated on a regular basis to make sure it still fits your needs and objectives.

Budgeting & Expense Management: It's critical to live within your means. Make a reasonable budget that covers both necessary and optional expenses. Keep tabs on your spending to find places where you may make savings without compromising your standard of living. Think about cutting back on luxury spending, downsizing your house, or locating more affordable options for your need.

Maximizing Revenue Sources: In retirement, consider every possible source of income. Apart from Social Security and pensions, take into account chances for freelance work or part-time job, property rentals, or converting pastimes into profitable ventures. Increasing the variety of your sources of income can help you feel more secure financially.

Postpone Social Security Benefits: You can get a substantial monthly payment boost if you postpone the commencement of your benefits. Long-term financial security can be achieved by delaying retiring until you reach your full retirement age or even beyond the age of 70, as your benefits will increase accordingly.

Handling Debt: Having no debt when you retire improves your financial stability. Prior to retirement, concentrate on paying off high-interest obligations like credit card balances and personal loans. Refinancing or combining debts could result in reduced interest rates and monthly payments.

Optimizing Revenue Sources: Examine every possible source of retirement income. Consider taking use of freelance or part-time work, property rentals, Social Security, pensions, and converting pastimes into sources of income in addition to Social Security. Getting the most out of several revenue sources helps increase financial security.

Postpone Social Security Benefits: Postponing the start of your Social Security benefits will result in a considerable boost in your monthly payments. Your benefits will be bigger and provide you greater long-term financial security if you can afford to wait until you reach full retirement age or even age 70.

Handling Debt: Reducing debt before retirement improves one's financial stability. Prioritize paying off high-interest obligations before you retire, such as personal loans and credit card bills. To reduce interest rates and monthly payments, think about refinancing or combining debts.

Seeking Professional Financial Advice: Speaking with a financial advisor can help you get insightful information and methods that are suited to your particular circumstances. A specialist can help you make the most of your resources, arrange for taxes, and improve your investment portfolio.

The Value of Investment Diversification

One of the most essential concepts in risk management for investments is diversification, which is particularly crucial in retirement.

Understanding diversification: To lower risk, diversification entails distributing investments among a variety of asset classes and industries, such as stocks, bonds, real estate, etc. By spreading out your investments, you lessen the effect of a single investment's bad performance on your portfolio as a whole.

Asset Allocation: Choose the right mix of assets according to your time horizon, financial objectives, and risk tolerance. Generally speaking, a more conservative allocation may be advised as you get closer to and into retirement to guard against market volatility. In comparison to equities, this usually signifies a larger percentage of bonds and lower-risk investments.

Frequent Portfolio Rebalancing: Market swings have the potential to cause your asset allocation to stray from your goal over time. To keep your preferred amount of risk in your portfolio, rebalance it on a regular basis. To achieve balance, this entails purchasing underperforming assets and selling overperforming ones.

Including Alternative Investments: For additional diversity, think about incorporating alternative investments like commodities, real estate, or REITs (Real Estate Investment Trusts). They can lessen dependency on the conventional stock and bond markets and offer other revenue streams.

Global Diversification: Diversification can be further improved by investing in foreign markets. Investing internationally might expose one to a variety of economic cycles and growth prospects that might not be accessible at home.

Dividend-Paying Stocks: Putting money into dividend-paying stocks now will help you generate a reliable retirement income later on. Dividends provide a safety net against market downturns and can be used to augment other sources of income.

Low-Cost Index Funds and ETFs: These exchange-traded funds (ETFs) and low-cost index funds provide extensive market exposure at a little cost. These can be important parts of a retirement portfolio and are effective diversification vehicles.

Emergency Savings and Preparedness

Even the best-laid financial plans can be derailed by unforeseen costs. In retirement, having an emergency fund and a backup plan is crucial to preserving financial stability.

How to Create an Emergency Fund: An emergency fund is a cash reserve put away for unforeseen bills, such house repairs, medical emergencies, or other unforeseen expenses. Try to keep three to six months' worth of living costs in an account that is easy to access, such a money market or savings account.

Creating the Fund Prior to Retirement: It is best to begin creating your emergency fund well in advance of retirement. Make consistent contributions to this fund, considering it an essential component of your spending plan. This guarantees you have a safety net in case your regular paycheck is discontinued.

Handling Medical Expenses: In retirement, medical costs can provide a substantial financial challenge. To help with the prospective costs of assisted living, in-home care, and nursing facilities, think about getting long-term care insurance. Examine and select Medicare plans that best fit your financial situation and medical requirements.

Planning for Major Expenses: Having a separate fund or plan for large anticipated needs, such a new car, house improvements, or major trip plans, is a good idea in addition to having an emergency reserve. This keeps you from having to take these expenses out of your emergency reserve or retirement funds.

Making a Contingency Plan: Make a plan that specifies what to do in the event of an unexpected financial situation. This could involve figuring out what assets you can sell, what credit lines you can get, or what costs you can reduce. A well-defined strategy mitigates anxiety and guarantees prompt response when required.

Examining Insurance Coverage: Part of emergency preparation is having enough insurance. Make sure you have enough coverage for health, house, vehicle, and life insurance by reviewing your plans. This guards against significant financial losses brought on by mishaps, medical conditions, or other unforeseen circumstances.

Legal and Estate Planning: Make sure you have all the necessary legal paperwork in order, including a power of attorney, will, and health care directive. These wills guarantee that your wishes are carried out in the event of your incapacity or death and safeguard your interests. Update them often to reflect any changes in your preferences or situation.

Keeping Up to Date and Flexible: Changes in the economy, the state of the market, or individual circumstances can cause the financial landscape to alter quickly. Keep up with current developments in finance and be prepared to modify your strategies as necessary. Navigating financial uncertainty requires flexibility.

Chapter 12
Handling Medical Concerns

One essential component of a happy retirement is good health. Proactively addressing health conditions can greatly improve your longevity and quality of life. This chapter explores the significance of mental health and well-being, proactive health management, and obtaining healthcare services and assistance.

Preventive Medical Care
In retirement, it's critical to manage your health proactively. This entails routine examinations, preventive care, adopting a healthy lifestyle, and maintaining up-to-date health knowledge.

Frequent Medical Check-Ups: It's important to get regular check-ups with your primary care physician and other specialists. Early identification and treatment of possible health problems are made possible by these visits. Regular screenings for common disorders including diabetes, cancer, and hypertension have to be a part of your healthcare regimen.

Preventive Care: By practicing preventive care, one can lower their chance of contracting chronic illnesses. This covers immunizations (such jabs against the flu and pneumonia), regular screenings (like mammograms and colonoscopies), and health evaluations (including tests for bone density and cholesterol). Early detection of problems allows for the best possible treatment.

Healthy Diet and Nutrition: A well-balanced diet consisting of fruits, vegetables, lean proteins, and whole grains is beneficial for general health. Diabetes, heart disease, and weight gain can all be avoided by limiting processed foods, carbohydrates, and saturated fats. A nutritionist's advice can help you customize a diet plan to meet your unique requirements.

Frequent Exercise: Maintaining an active lifestyle is essential to good physical health. Frequent exercise helps preserve muscle mass, increase flexibility, and improve cardiovascular health. Examples of this type of exercise include swimming, yoga, strength training, and walking. Try to get in at least 150 minutes a week of moderate activity.

Weight management: Retaining a healthy weight lowers the chance of heart disease, diabetes, and joint complications, among other health problems. To properly maintain weight, combine regular exercise with a nutritious diet. Keeping an eye on your body mass index, or BMI, can help you determine a healthy weight.

Sufficient Sleep: Both physical and mental well-being depend on getting enough good sleep. Try to get seven to nine hours each night. Maintaining a regular sleep schedule, setting up a peaceful environment, and abstaining from stimulants right before bed are examples of good sleep hygiene practices.

Stress management: Prolonged stress can have a negative impact on one's health and cause diseases including anxiety, depression, and hypertension. Include stress-relieving pursuits in your daily routine, such as hobbies, deep breathing techniques, meditation, and quality time spent with loved ones.

Avoiding Bad Habits: Steer clear of bad habits like smoking and binge drinking. Reducing alcohol consumption and quitting smoking can both have a major positive impact on health.

Getting Support and Resources for Healthcare

It can be difficult to navigate the healthcare system and obtain the tools you need, but doing so is essential to properly managing health conditions.

Knowing Medicare and Medicaid: Become knowledgeable about Medicare, Medicaid, and more health care programs. For anyone over 65 or with specific disabilities, Medicare offers health insurance that covers doctor visits, hospital stays, and prescription medication. Medicaid helps people with low incomes pay for medical expenses. Gaining knowledge about your eligibility and benefits will enable you to get the most out of these initiatives.

Choosing the Correct Healthcare Providers: Pick medical professionals that have expertise handling the health problems that are typical of older persons. For example, a geriatrician specializes in the treatment of elderly patients and can offer comprehensive care that is customized to meet your needs.

Using Telehealth Services: These services, which provide easy access to medical consultations and follow-ups from the comfort of your home, are becoming more and more popular. This is particularly helpful for regular check-ups.

Pharmacy Services: A lot of pharmacies provide services like health screenings, vaccinations, and medication management. To ensure that you utilize medications safely and efficiently, pharmacists can offer helpful information on how to take medications and any interactions.

Community Health Resources: Exercise programs, health seminars, and support groups are among the health resources frequently offered by neighborhood community centers, senior centers, and nonprofit organizations. Engaging in these kinds of activities can improve your health and give you a sense of belonging.

Health Insurance: To effectively manage healthcare costs, be sure you have enough coverage. This could involve long-term care insurance to help with costs associated with impairments or chronic illnesses, or supplemental insurance to fill in Medicare's gaps.

Health Apps and Wearables: Utilize wearables and health apps to track and manage your health. Wearable technology and health apps can monitor vital signs, exercise, sleep patterns, and other things. These gadgets can warn you about possible health problems and offer real-time feedback.

Value of Mental Health and Overall Well-Being

Particularly after retirement, mental and physical well-being are equally crucial. Sustaining your mental health can greatly improve your life's quality.

Mental Health Awareness: Acknowledge the need of maintaining good mental health and be informed on prevalent problems including anxiety, depression, and cognitive decline. To preserve a high quality of life, mental health concerns must be identified early and treated.

Maintaining Social relationships: Maintaining social relationships is essential for mental health. Regularly interact with friends, family, and neighborhood organizations. Social connections help lessen depressive and lonely feelings, which are risk factors for mental health problems.

Taking Part in Meaningful Activities: Look for interests and pursuits that make you happy and fulfilled. Taking part in activities you enjoy, such as volunteering, traveling, drawing, or gardening, can improve your mental and emotional well-being.

Mental Stimulation: Engage in lifelong learning and mental activities to keep your mind sharp. Games, puzzles, reading, and picking up new knowledge or abilities can all support cognitive function and stave off cognitive decline.

Mindfulness and Relaxation Methods: To reduce stress and improve mental clarity, engage in mindfulness, meditation, and relaxation methods. These techniques can elevate mood, lessen tension, and foster tranquility and wellbeing.

Professional Support: If you require professional assistance, don't be afraid to ask for it. Support groups, therapists, and counselors can all be very helpful in managing mental health concerns. Therapy can assist in addressing emotional difficulties and creating coping mechanisms.

Healthy Relationships: Maintaining and cultivating good connections is important. Good relationships lower stress, offer emotional support, and enhance happiness in general. Improve your ability to communicate and settle disputes in order to improve your relationships.

Physical Activity for Mental Health: Engaging in regular physical activity promotes both physical and mental well-being. Exercise releases endorphins, which have been shown to elevate mood and lessen anxiety and depressive symptoms.

Balanced Lifestyle: Make an effort to lead a balanced life that allows for work, relaxation, and recreation. Maintaining balance in your daily schedule can help you avoid burnout and make time for things that are good for your mental and emotional well-being.

Access to Mental Health Resources: Become acquainted with the resources that are accessible for mental health. Numerous organizations provide local support services, internet resources, and hotlines that can be of assistance when needed.

Proactively managing one's physical and mental well-being is essential when dealing with health concerns throughout retirement. Retirees can greatly improve their quality of life and overall health by making routine check-ups, preventive care, leading a healthy lifestyle, and being aware of the services that are available to them a priority. A healthy and meaningful retirement can be maintained by concentrating on your mental health and well-being in addition to accessing healthcare services and support to guarantee you receive the required care. Retirees can confidently and resiliently navigate the health challenges of retirement with careful planning and proactive management.

Chapter 13

Accepting Modifications in Lifestyle

The move to retirement is a momentous occasion that alters a person's daily schedule, sense of purpose, and way of life in general. It takes flexibility, receptivity to new experiences, and a proactive approach to reinventing your life to get through this phase successfully. The significance of adjusting to a new daily schedule, discovering new interests and purposes, and accepting change and flexibility are all covered in this chapter.

Getting Used to a New Daily Schedule

Making the shift from an organized career to an unstructured retirement may be both freeing and difficult. Creating a new daily routine contributes to the maintenance of structure and purpose, both of which are essential for mental and physical health.

Establishing a Daily routine: Although not needing an alarm clock before retiring, a loose daily routine can offer much-needed structure. Make time in your schedule for a variety of pursuits, including hobbies, physical activity, socializing, and rest. A fulfilling lifestyle is encouraged and emotions of aimlessness are lessened thanks to this balance.

Morning Routines: Developing a reliable morning schedule helps brighten the remainder of the day. This can entail doing things like doing out in the morning, reading the news, eating a balanced breakfast, and practicing mindfulness techniques like journaling or meditation.

Physical Activity: Maintaining your health and vigor requires that you engage in frequent physical activity. Getting moving, whether it's through a yoga class, a gym visit, or a daily stroll, improves mood, vitality, and general wellbeing.

Mental Stimulation: Mental activity is equally as vital as physical activity. Set aside time each day for mentally taxing pursuits like reading, solving puzzles, picking up new skills, or participating in thought-provoking conversations. By doing this, mental deterioration can be avoided and cognitive function can be preserved.

Social Interaction: Include social events on a daily basis in your schedule. Plan frequent get-togethers with loved ones, take part in group activities, and/or join clubs and associations that pique your interest. To prevent loneliness and foster a sense of community, social connection is essential.

Interests & Hobbies: Make time for the pursuit of interests and hobbies that make you happy and content. Participating in things you love, such as cooking, painting, gardening, or playing an instrument, can improve your quality of life and give you a sense of accomplishment.

Rest and Relaxation: Make sure to schedule time for rest and relaxation in your daily schedule. Retirement offers the chance to do things more slowly and savor life more thoroughly. Spend some time relaxing, whether it's by reading, watching TV, napping, or spending time in nature.

Volunteering & Giving Back: Giving back to the community is a fulfilling activity for many retirees. Engaging in volunteer work can offer a feeling of direction, chances for interpersonal communication, and the fulfillment that comes from supporting a cause you are passionate about.

Discovering New Interests and Purposes

Retirement is a great opportunity to find new hobbies and revisit long-lost ones. Maintaining a sense of fulfillment and joy in this new stage of life requires discovering new passions and purposes.

Self-Discovery: Take this opportunity to discover what genuinely fascinates and intrigues you. Think back on your prior knowledge, abilities, and interests. Think on the things that made you happy or made you lose sight of time. Finding new topics to investigate can be aided by this self-discovery process.

Establishing Goals: Goal-setting is crucial for motivation and personal development even after retirement. These objectives may pertain to personal projects, travel, education, or health. A goal or objective can give one a feeling of purpose and accomplishment.

Lifelong Learning: Retirement is the ideal time to continue your education. Take classes, go to workshops, or start a new pastime. Numerous community centers and institutions provide programs especially for retirees. Acquiring new knowledge maintains mental acuity and creates opportunities for novel experiences and satisfaction.

Travel and Place Exploration: A lot of retirees like taking trips and discovering new locations. Traveling can offer fresh perspectives, exciting new encounters, and a wider range of activities, whether you're talking about national parks, local day outings, or foreign adventures.

Creative Activities: Take part in artistic endeavors that give you the chance to express yourself. This could be achieved through crafts, music, writing, or art. Being creative can be incredibly fulfilling and therapeutic, providing a constructive outlet for your feelings and thoughts.

Community Involvement: Participating in your local community may be a highly rewarding experience. Join community clubs, take part in local events, or carry out civic duties. Participating in this can give one a feeling of purpose and belonging.

Mentoring and expertise Sharing: A lot of retirees find fulfillment in passing on their skills and expertise to others. This could be accomplished through official mentorship programs, unofficial advice, or classroom instruction. Giving to others can be a deeply fulfilling and enduring way to make a difference.

Family Engagement: Make time for your loved ones, especially your grandchildren. In addition to giving them a feeling of purpose and happiness, being actively involved in their lives helps improve family ties. Take part in activities, exchange tales, and make enduring memories with one another.

Accepting Adaptability and Change

Retirement is a period of great transition, and the secret to enjoying this new phase of life is to learn to be flexible. Retirement can be richer and more fulfilling if you're willing to try new things and change with the times.

Open-Mindedness: Have an open mind as you approach retirement. Be open to trying out new things, getting to know new people, and discovering new hobbies. Having an open mind can improve your life and present you with unexpected chances.

Adaptability: Things might not always go according to plan when you retire. Unexpected circumstances, changes in finances, or health problems could arise. You can find new ways forward and deal with these challenges by developing your adaptability. Have an adaptable mentality and be ready to modify your plans when circumstances demand.

Positivity: It's important to keep an optimistic outlook when things are changing. Pay more attention to the opportunities and possibilities that retirement offers than to its drawbacks. Your resilience can be strengthened and you can face problems with grace if you are positive.

Making Connections with Other Retirees: Gain knowledge from their experiences. Join online forums or retirement communities to exchange experiences, counsel, and encouragement. Acquiring knowledge from others can yield significant perspectives and motivation.

Finding a Balance Between Structure and Spontaneity

While following a routine is crucial, make time for spontaneity as well. Accept the flexibility to act spontaneously, whether it's booking a last-minute trip, dining at a new place, or going to an unplanned event. Your life can become more exciting and varied with this balance.

Using Technology: You can have a far better retirement experience with technology. Utilize it to manage your finances, pick up new skills, discover new hobbies, and maintain relationships with loved ones. You may stay informed and involved by keeping an open mind to emerging technologies.

Retrospection and Adjustment: Take time to consider your retirement experience and make any necessary adjustments. Evaluate what's functioning well and what needs to be improved. Making adjustments on your own will guarantee that your retirement is meaningful and in line with your objectives.

Seeking Support: If you're having trouble making the switch to retirement, don't be afraid to ask for help. Talking to friends and relatives, attending support groups, or counseling could all help with this. For people to manage change and preserve their mental and emotional health, support networks are essential.

Adapting to a new daily schedule, discovering new interests and purposes, and being adaptable and open to change are all part of embracing lifestyle adjustments in retirement. Creating a balanced schedule gives life direction and enhances general health. Setting objectives and pursuing new hobbies helps you stay fulfilled and motivated. You can better handle the unavoidable changes and difficulties that come with this new stage of life by learning to be flexible and adaptable. You may design a fulfilling and pleasurable retirement experience by adopting a proactive and optimistic outlook.

Chapter 14

Is It Time for Me to Retire?

For many people, the idea of retiring early—that is, before the customary retirement age of 65—is an ambition. It's a choice that needs careful analysis of the advantages and disadvantages, the financial ramifications, and lifestyle and health factors. To assist you decide if an early retirement is the correct decision for you, this chapter goes into great detail about these aspects.

Analyzing the Benefits and Drawbacks of Early Retirement

Benefits of Early Retirement

More Personal Time: Taking an early retirement gives you more time for travel, hobbies, and socializing with loved ones. A life that is richer and more satisfying may result from this.

Better Health and Wellness: Early retirement from the workforce can lower stress and enhance general health. You've got more time.

Possibility for New Interests: An early retirement gives the opportunity to investigate voluntary work, entrepreneurship, or alternative vocations. It's a chance to pursue interests and passions that might not have been possible while working a full-time job.

Spending More Time with Family and Friends: An early retirement enables you to make more time for your partner, kids, grandchildren, and friends. This can improve bonds between people and produce priceless memories.

Flexibility and Freedom: You are free to live your life as you see fit, free from the demands of a job schedule. This adaptability might improve your general contentment and pleasure.

Drawbacks of Early Retirement

Financial Pressure: Making sure you have adequate savings to support yourself for a longer period of time is one of the main obstacles of retiring early. This calls for discipline and cautious budgeting.

Possibility of Boredom: Some retirees may experience boredom or a feeling of aimlessness in the absence of the structure and purpose that work offers. It is imperative to engage in worthwhile activities to pass the time.

Social Isolation: A person's social connections frequently take place mostly at work. If an individual does not establish a robust social network beyond their occupation, retiring at an early age may result in feelings of loneliness.

Effect on Benefits: Retiring early may have an impact on your ability to receive employer-sponsored health insurance, pensions, and Social Security benefits. Making an informed choice requires having a thorough understanding of these effects.

Market Risk and Inflation: Retiring early exposes you to inflation and market volatility because it forces you to rely on your savings and investments for a longer amount of time. To reduce risks, this calls for a sound financial plan.

The Financial Costs of Early Retirement
Evaluating Your Level of Financial Prepareness

Savings and assets: Assess your present savings and assets to see if you have enough to sustain your desired standard of living for at least the next thirty years. To determine your needs, use retirement calculators and financial advisor consultations.

Income Streams: List all of your sources of income, including Social Security, pensions, retirement funds (401(k), IRA), and any other investments. To lower risk, make sure you have a variety of revenue sources.

Budgeting: Make a thorough retirement plan that accounts for all necessary expenditures, as well as discretionary cash and future medical needs. To make sure your budget stays reasonable over time, account for inflation.

Debt management: Try to have as little debt as possible when you retire. Your retirement assets can be rapidly depleted by high-interest debt, which makes it more difficult to maintain financial stability.

Recognizing the Effects of Social Security and Pensions

Social Security: You won't be able to get payments from Social Security if you retire before the age of sixty-two. Even yet, if benefits are taken early rather than waiting until full retirement age or later, the monthly amount will be smaller.

Pensions: Be aware of the guidelines for early retirement if you have a pension plan. Certain plans have lower benefits if you retire ahead of schedule.

Insurance and Medical Expenses

Healthcare Coverage: You will require private health insurance if you are under 65 because you will not be eligible for Medicare before that age. You should set aside money for premiums, deductibles, and out-of-pocket costs because this can get pricey.

Long-term Care: Think about whether you'll need long-term care and how you'll pay for it. Protecting your savings with long-term care insurance may prove to be a wise investment.

Tax-Related Issues

Tax-efficient Withdrawals: To reduce your tax obligations, schedule your retirement account withdrawals in a way that will minimize taxes. To minimize your tax burden, think about the sequence in which you take withdrawals from various accounts.

Roth Conversions: Examine the advantages of converting money from a standard IRA or 401(k) to a Roth IRA. This can lower required minimum distributions and generate tax-free income in retirement.

A Look at Health and Lifestyle

Preserving Physical Well-Being

Frequent Exercise: Make physical activity a frequent part of your day. Exercise is essential for preserving physical well-being, lowering stress levels, and averting chronic illnesses.

Healthy Diet: Pay attention to a wholesome, well-balanced diet. A healthy diet promotes general well-being and helps ward against many age-related ailments.

Frequent Check-ups: Keep track of your health's annual physicals and screenings. By using preventive healthcare, you can stay healthy for longer and identify possible problems early.

Emotional and Mental Health

Mental Stimulation: Take part in mentally taxing activities like reading, solving puzzles, picking up new skills, or picking up new interests. Cognitive function is maintained through mental stimulation.

Social Engagement: Continue to have close social ties. Engage in community events, volunteer work, or join clubs to maintain social interaction and fight loneliness.

Meaning and Fulfillment: Look for pursuits that give you a feeling of fulfillment and meaning. This might include taking up a passion project, mentoring others, or volunteering.

Creating a Network of Support

Friends and Family: Maintain your relationships with friends and family. Good relationships are essential for general happiness and emotional support.

Participate in the Community: Engage with the people in your neighborhood. Join clubs or associations that share your values and areas of interest.

Professional Support: If you require professional assistance, don't be afraid to ask for it. Financial consultants, medical specialists, and mental health counselors are a few examples of this.

Getting Used to Shifting Lifestyles

Flexible Mindset: Be adaptable and receptive to change. Unexpected possibilities and problems can arise during retirement; a flexible mentality will help you effectively navigate them.

New Routines: Create fresh, purposeful, and structured routines. This might keep you interested and help avoid boredom.

Exploration & Discovery: Make the most of this opportunity to delve into new pursuits and uncover your passions. Taking an early retirement gives you the chance to start over and write a successful second act.

Choosing to retire early is a difficult and very private choice. It necessitates a serious analysis of the benefits and drawbacks, a detailed comprehension of the financial ramifications, and a deliberate consideration of lifestyle and health-related issues. You may make an informed choice that fits your objectives, values, and situation by using a comprehensive strategy and careful planning.

Early retirement can present a wealth of chances for leisure, personal development, and travel. It does, however, also entail hazards and difficulties that must be properly handled. Maintaining one's physical, mental, and emotional well-being is just as important as being financially prepared. Developing a robust support system and maintaining an open mind to novel experiences can augment your early retirement adventure.

The choice to retire early should ultimately be supported by a realistic evaluation of your financial condition, a clear sense of your objectives and aspirations, and a readiness to welcome the opportunities and adjustments that accompany this momentous life transformation. An exciting new chapter in your life might be opened up by an early retirement with proper planning and aggressive measures.

Chapter 15

Advantages of Taking Early Retirement

Beyond the obvious financial and leisure rewards, early retirement can be a life-changing experience with many advantages. The chance to pursue goals and new hobbies, better general health and lower stress levels, and the advantages of simplifying and downsizing are just a few of the major benefits that are covered in this chapter.

Enhanced General Health and Decreased Stress Advantages for Physical Health

Early retirement can have a significant effect on physical well-being. Workday tedium frequently leaves little time for rest, exercise, and a good diet. People can put their health first by retiring early and doing the following:

Enhanced Physical Activity: Retirees who have more spare time might partake in regular physical activities like yoga, running, walking, or swimming. Maintaining cardiovascular health, controlling weight, and lowering the risk of chronic illnesses like diabetes and hypertension all depend on regular exercise.

Improved Sleep Patterns: Work-related stress and demands can cause sleep patterns to be disturbed. Early retirees frequently discover that they may create a more regular sleep schedule that is both peaceful and consistent—a critical component of good health.

Better Eating Practices: Retirees can concentrate on a healthy diet full of fruits, vegetables, whole grains, and lean proteins now that they have more time to cook at home. Making meals at home also lessens the need for fast food and packaged foods.

Frequent Health Check-ups: Those who retire early are free to arrange and attend routine medical visits without being constrained by a job schedule. Early detection and treatment of possible health problems are made possible by this proactive approach to healthcare.

Advantages for Mental Health

Equally important are the advantages early retirement has for mental health. Improving mental health is facilitated by the opportunity to focus on personal well-being and the decrease of work-related stress:

Decreased Stress Levels: Prolonged stress has a detrimental effect on mental health and can be brought on by job conflicts, performance reviews, and deadline pressure. These pressures are eliminated by early retirement, enabling a more carefree and tranquil existence.

Increased Leisure Time: Taking part in enjoyable and fulfilling hobbies and leisure pursuits might improve mental health. Playing an instrument, gardening, or painting are examples of hobbies that bring one a sense of purpose and accomplishment.

Better Social Connections: Retirees who leave early have more time to cultivate friendships and family ties. Social connections, which offer companionship, support, and a sense of belonging, are essential for mental health.

Personal Development and Education: Retirement provides the chance to explore new passions and lifetime education. The mind is kept active and engaged when it is involved in educational pursuits, whether through self-study or formal classes.

Possibility of Following Dreams and Trying New Things

The ability to pursue goals and interests that may have been postponed owing to work obligations is made possible by early retirement. This increased independence may result in a richer and more satisfying life:

Journeying and Investigating

Extended Travel: Retirees are free to take long trips without being restricted by the number of vacation days they have available. One's perspective can be expanded and found immense satisfaction in discovering other cultures, sceneries, and experiences.

Cultural and Adventure Travel: An early retirement provides the time and freedom to pursue a variety of travel activities, such as going to historical sites, attending local celebrations, or participating in adventure sports.

Interests and Feelings

Creative Activities: Painting, writing, photography, handicraft, and other creative endeavors might be pursued during an early retirement. Engaging in these pursuits can offer immense fulfillment and a feeling of accomplishment.

Volunteering and Community Service: Giving back to the community is a fulfilling activity for many retirees. Volunteering for issues one is enthusiastic about can give one a sense of direction and have a beneficial effect.

Learning and Education: Going back to school after retirement is a great idea. Learning new talents, learning a new language, or enrolling in classes at the local college are all examples of how ongoing education keeps the mind active and sharp.

Business Initiatives

Launching a Business: Taking an early retirement may present a chance to launch a small company or engage in other entrepreneurial endeavors. Retirees can transform their hobbies into successful businesses by founding a café, consulting practice, or online store.

Investing in Passions: Retirement can involve retirees in pastimes like carpentry, gardening, or handicraft that might provide cash. Creating a career out of a passion can be financially advantageous as well as fulfilling.

Reducing and streamlining one's life

People who retire early frequently have to reevaluate their lifestyles and give downsizing and simplifying a thought. This change may have a number of advantages:

Economic Advantages

Reduce Living expenditures: You can drastically cut living expenditures by moving to a more cheap area or downsizing to a smaller home. This can lessen the burden on retirement savings and free up cash for other goals.

Decreased Maintenance: Living in a smaller home or leading a simpler lifestyle can save money and effort. This frees up retirees to concentrate on hobbies and pastimes rather than maintenance and housework.

Decluttering and Simplifying: Reducing the amount of belongings supports these two actions. A living space that is less chaotic and more ordered can result from minimizing material possessions.

Lifestyle Advantages

More Flexibility: You'll have more freedom to follow your interests and hobbies if you simplify your life and take on fewer obligations. Retirees have more time to travel and explore since they are not burdened with the maintenance of a large home or the management of multiple assets.

Improved Life Quality: Living a simpler lifestyle is frequently associated with a higher quality of life. Experiences, as opposed to material belongings, might provide greater happiness and fulfillment.

Environmental Impact: Reducing and streamlining can also benefit the environment. Living more sustainably and with a lesser carbon impact is made possible by smaller housing and lower consumption.

Chapter 16

Overcoming Retirement-Related Fear

Whether it's early or typical retirement age, there's always a mixture of anticipation and anxiety. It's normal to be scared and anxious about such a big change in life. This chapter discusses common retirement anxieties, offers strategies for reducing stress and anxiety, and delves into the idea of Sudden Retirement Syndrome (SRS).

Resolving Typical Retirement Fears
Apprehension about financial instability

The worry that one would outlive their savings is one of the most common anxieties among retirees. To deal with this anxiety:

Financial Planning: Create a thorough financial plan that consists of a thorough budget, a withdrawal strategy, and a backup plan in case of unforeseen costs. You can feel more at ease and make sure your finances are in order by speaking with a financial counselor.

Diversified Investments: To reduce risk, make sure your portfolio of investments is diverse. Growth and stability can be attained with a well-diversified portfolio of stocks, bonds, and other assets.

Emergency Fund: Set aside money for unforeseen costs in your emergency fund. Anxiety around unanticipated financial difficulties might be reduced by having a safety net.

Fear of Losing Identity and Purpose

Identity and purpose are frequently given by one's work. To get past this fear:

Find New Purpose: Choose interests and pursuits that make you happy and fulfilled in order to discover your new purpose. A sense of purpose can be attained by volunteering, taking up hobbies, or performing community service.

Set Objectives: Make fresh objectives and tasks to strive toward. Having objectives can offer your days structure and significance, whether they are related to finishing a house makeover, publishing a book, or learning a new skill.

Stay Involved: Continue to engage in social activities and cultivate new contacts. Social interaction and participation in events can strengthen your feeling of self and identity.

Fear of Being Alone and Bored

Feelings of loneliness and boredom can occasionally accompany retirement. To counteract this:

Keep Moving: Take part in enjoyable physical activities. Getting involved in sports, dancing courses, or gym memberships might help you stay socially and physically active.

Explore Interests: Take up new interests or revive previous ones. Playing an instrument, painting, or gardening are examples of hobbies that can bring happiness and a sense of success.

Join Clubs and Groups: Join groups or clubs whose objectives coincide with your own. This can facilitate social contact and make things easier.

Strategies for Reducing Stress and Anxiety
Techniques for Relaxation and Mindfulness

Meditation: Meditation is a useful tool for promoting calmness and lowering anxiety. Every day, set aside some time to meditate and pay attention to your breathing.

Yoga and Tai Chi: These forms of exercise combine mindfulness with physical activity to help lower stress and enhance mental clarity.

Simple deep breathing techniques may be performed anywhere and are an effective way to reduce tension and anxiety.

Organizing Process

Daily Routine: Make time each day for hobbies, physical activity, social interactions, and rest. A well-planned routine can give one a feeling of purpose and normalcy.

Typical Tasks: Schedule frequent events and excursions. A monthly book club, a weekly coffee date with friends, or a daily walk, regular activities can provide stability and enjoyment.

Expert Assistance

Counselors and therapists: Consulting a mental health professional for support can be helpful. They can offer advice on how to deal with worry and help during the retirement transition.

Support Groups: Becoming a member of a retirement support group helps foster understanding and a sense of community. Talking about your experiences with people who are going through similar changes can be enlightening and consoling.

The Theory of Unexpected Retirement (SRS)

The phrase "Sudden Retirement Syndrome" (SRS) refers to the emotional and psychological difficulties that some people experience after retiring suddenly. Gaining an understanding of SRS will help you successfully plan for and handle these issues.

Signs and symptoms of SRS

Anxiety and Depression: As people come to terms with losing their professional identity and routine, feelings of anxiety, melancholy, or depression may surface.

Restlessness and irritation: When they struggle to occupy their time and find new meaning, retirees may experience restlessness, irritation, or a sense of anxiety.

Sleep Disturbances: Sleep problems, such as insomnia or abnormal sleep patterns, can be brought on by stress and changes in daily routine.

Techniques for Reducing SRS

Gradual Transition: If it's feasible, think about retiring gradually. A phased retirement plan or part-time employment can facilitate the transition.

Pre-retirement Planning: Make plans for your future that take into account not just your financial situation but also your social and psychological needs. Consider your time management strategy and the activities that will bring you joy.

Remain Involved: Continue to be involved in worthwhile endeavors. This can involve taking part in community events, volunteering, or learning new skills.

Seek Assistance: Never be afraid to ask for help from friends, family, or experts. Navigating the emotional side of retirement might be made easier by sharing your experiences and feelings.

Accepting a Novel Phase

Positivity: Adopt an optimistic outlook as you approach retirement. Pay more attention to the potential it presents than the losses. Seize the opportunity to pursue new hobbies and have more spare time.

Lifelong Learning: Make learning a priority in your life. Learning new talents or enrolling in new classes can stimulate the mind and give one a sense of achievement.

Celebrate Milestones: Honor significant anniversaries and accomplishments along the way to retirement. Acknowledge and value the strides you take to get used to this new chapter of life.

Numerous advantages of early retirement include better health, lower stress levels, and the chance to explore new interests and aspirations. It also offers an opportunity to simplify and minimize, which can improve general wellbeing. But it's normal to be scared and anxious about such a big shift in one's life. You can overcome these obstacles and welcome a happy and satisfying retirement by addressing typical retirement worries, using techniques to reduce stress and anxiety, and comprehending ideas like Sudden Retirement Syndrome.

To overcome your fear of retirement and make the most of this exciting new chapter in your life, prepare yourself, have a good outlook, and take proactive steps to engage in things that give you joy and purpose.

Chapter 17

Relocating to an assisted living facility

Relocating to a retirement community can provide retirees with a nurturing and fulfilling environment as they enter a new stage of their lives. The benefits of retirement communities, their various varieties, and how to choose the best one for your needs are all covered in this chapter.

Retirement Communities' Benefits
Activities and Social Engagement

Retirement communities provide a variety of activities and are built to encourage social interactions.

Social Interaction: The integrated social network is one of the main advantages. Frequent social connection with peers can improve general well-being by lowering emotions of isolation and loneliness.

Structured Activities: Fitness courses, painting classes, gardening groups, and cultural excursions are just a few of the organized activities that are available in many communities. Engaging in these activities offers chances to learn new things, maintain an active lifestyle, and pursue hobbies.

Events and Gatherings: To foster a lively social environment, retirement homes frequently organize events and gatherings including movie evenings, community dinners, and holiday celebrations.

Convenient Amenities and Services

A variety of facilities and services are offered by retirement communities to improve daily convenience:

Maintenance-Free Living: By providing maintenance services like housekeeping, landscaping, and home repairs, many communities enable its residents to lead worry-free lives.

Healthcare Services: Residents can obtain prompt medical care and support if they have access to on-site healthcare services or nearby medical facilities.

Dining Options: A lot of retirement homes include dining areas with wholesome meals that can accommodate a range of dietary requirements and preferences. This can ensure that seniors keep a balanced diet and lessen the strain of preparing meals.

Transportation Services: To give residents more mobility and independence, communities frequently offer transportation for shopping, doctor visits, and leisure trips.

Increased Security and Safety

In retirement communities, security and safety come first:

Around-the-clock Security: To protect its citizens, several communities have monitoring systems and security guards on duty. Security is further improved with emergency response systems and gated access.

Emergency Assistance: Residents and their family can feel secure knowing that in the event of a medical emergency or other emergency, on-site staff and emergency call systems will respond immediately.

Community Layout: Well-lit pathways, handrails, and accessible amenities are just a few examples of the safety-enhancing elements that are frequently incorporated into retirement community designs.

Retirement Community Types
Communities of Independent Living

Active seniors who can manage their everyday tasks but desire a community atmosphere are catered to by independent living communities:

Active Lifestyle: Residents of these communities can maintain an active and social lifestyle by participating in a variety of recreational.

Private Residences: Tenants have access to shared facilities including dining halls, exercise centers, and recreation areas from their private apartments or homes.

Minimal Assistance: Although these communities offer a helping atmosphere, they usually don't give a lot of personal or medical care services.

Communities of Assisted Living

Seniors in assisted living facilities receive assistance with everyday tasks:

Personal Care Services: Help is on hand to help with activities including dressing, bathing, taking medications, and preparing meals.

Healthcare Access: To meet the health needs of its people, these communities frequently have healthcare professionals on site or have agreements with surrounding medical facilities.

Social and Recreational Activities: To keep residents involved, assisted living communities provide social and recreational activities, even with their greater level of care.

Retirement Communities with Continuing Care (CCRCs)

A continuum of care is provided by CCRCs, allowing residents to have their needs changed over time.

Comprehensive Care Levels: CCRCs offer skilled nursing care, independent living, and assisted living, enabling residents to move smoothly as their medical needs change.

Long-Term Stability: Residents can continue to live in the same community and get regular assistance and care, which offers security and comfort.

Financial Models: Depending on the degree of care and services offered, CCRCs frequently charge an admission fee as well as monthly fees.

Professional Nursing Facilities

Individuals with severe medical illnesses get intense medical care from skilled nursing institutions, sometimes referred to as nursing homes:

Medical Services: For people with complicated medical needs, these facilities provide round-the-clock medical care, rehabilitation services, and aid with everyday tasks.

Short-Term and Long-Term Care: Both short-term patients undergoing rehabilitation and long-term residents in need of continuous medical care are served by skilled nursing facilities.

Specialized Care: Certain facilities focus on particular kinds of care, such memory care for people with Alzheimer's or dementia.

Choosing the Ideal Community for Your Requirements Evaluating Individual

Requirements and Choices

Health and Care Needs: Assess your present state of health as well as any possible needs down the road. Think about areas that provide the right caliber of medical attention and services.

Activities and Lifestyle: Consider the way of life you wish to lead. Seek out neighborhoods with amenities and activities that suit your tastes and areas of interest.

Location & Proximity: Take into account the community's proximity to friends, relatives, and medical professionals. Nearby to be adored and medical facilities can be crucial.

Investigating and Observing Communities

Internet Research: Look into communities first. To gain an idea of what each town has to offer, read reviews, check out websites, and take virtual tours.

In-Person Visits: Arrange to visit multiple communities to get a firsthand look. To get a sense of the community's vibe, visit the facilities, talk to the employees and residents, and take part in events.

Questions to Pose: Make a list of inquiries you would like to make while there. Ask questions concerning medical services, social events, restaurants, safety precautions, and prices.

Analyzing Financial Options and Expenses

Cost Structure: Recognize the entry fees, monthly dues, and any extra expenses for extra services and facilities associated with each community.

Budgeting: Evaluate your financial status and think about speaking with a financial expert. Make certain that the community you choose fits within your budget and long-term financial plan.

Contracts and Agreements: Go over contracts and agreements carefully to make sure you understand all of the terms and circumstances, including any guarantees about future care and return procedures.

Chapter 18

Maintaining Relationships with Friends and Family

Retaining close bonds with friends and family is necessary for a happy retirement. This chapter looks at ways to stay in touch with people using technology, forging new friendships and social networks, and preserving existing ones.

Techniques for Sustaining Partnerships
Frequent Exchange of Information

Scheduled Visits and Calls: Make it a habit to speak with loved ones and friends on a regular basis. Scheduled visits and phone or video chats on a weekly or biweekly basis help maintain solid ties.

Family Get-Togethers: To preserve strong ties, schedule get-togethers and reunions. Birthdays, holidays, and other special occasions are great chances to gather everyone together.

Emails and Letters: Sending emails and letters to loved ones who might not be as tech-savvy can be a heartfelt way to stay in touch.

Engaged Engagement

Attend Events: Take part in milestones, festivities, and family get-togethers. Attending significant events forges deeper bonds and produces enduring memories.

Shared Activities: Take part in hobbies or pastimes with your loved ones, like cooking, gardening, or going to cultural events. Deeper ties are fostered by shared experiences.

Provide Support: Show your family and friends that you are there for them. Relationships can be strengthened by lending a sympathetic ear or a helping hand when required.

Honest Communication

Express Emotions: Be honest in your communication about your emotions and experiences. A genuine and trustworthy friendship is facilitated by sharing your views and feelings.

Resolve Conflicts: Take swift, proactive measures to resolve disagreements or misunderstandings. Relationship damage can be avoided by using effective communication and dispute resolution techniques.

Express Gratitude: Make sure to thank and show appreciation for your loved ones on a regular basis. Strong bonds can be maintained with little acts of kindness like kind presents or messages of appreciation.

Creating New Social Networks and Friends
Joining Associations and Clubs

Local Clubs: Get involved in neighborhood groups or clubs that share your interests, such exercise classes, literature clubs, or gardening clubs. These environments offer chances to connect with people who share your interests.

Volunteer Groups: Engaging in volunteer work for causes close to your heart not only benefits the community but also fosters relationships with like-minded individuals.

Senior Centers: Senior centers can be found in many towns, providing a range of programs and activities. By taking part in these initiatives, you can make new acquaintances.

Taking Part in Community Activities

Community Events: Participate in neighborhood get-togethers, fairs, and festivals. These are great occasions to interact with your community and meet new people.

Workshops and Classes: Sign up for any local workshops or classes that are being offered. These events, which can include culinary classes, art workshops, or educational seminars, can help you make new acquaintances.

Religious or Spiritual Groups: Attending church or a temple might be a sign of your religious or spiritual beliefs.

Social media and online communities

Social Media Sites: Make new acquaintances and maintain relationships with old pals by using social media sites like

LinkedIn, Instagram, and Facebook. Join communities and groups that you find interesting.

Online Forums: Take part in discussion boards and online forums according to your interests and hobbies. You can interact with individuals worldwide through these channels.

Virtual Meetups: Participate in online events and virtual meetups. You can meet new people and take part in discussions virtually at meetup.com and other websites.

Technology-Assisted Staying In Touch
Chat apps and video calls

Video Call Platforms: To conduct in-person chats with loved ones who live far away, use video call platforms like Zoom, Skype, and FaceTime.

Chat Apps: For immediate communication, use chat apps like Facebook Messenger, Viber, and WhatsApp. You can quickly send text messages, images, and videos with these apps.

Group conversations: To communicate and exchange updates, start group conversations with your loved ones. Using group conversations to keep everyone informed can be entertaining.

Social Networks

Facebook: Share updates, interact with friends and family, and join groups and events on Facebook. Facebook also has texting and video calling capabilities.

Instagram: Post images and videos from your day-to-day activities on Instagram. With the help of pictures and narratives, you may maintain connections on this visual platform.

LinkedIn: This is a terrific place to network and maintain contact with old coworkers and other professionals.

Calendars on the Internet and Email

Email correspondence: Send longer updates or more official correspondence via email. It's a dependable method of communication, particularly with folks who might not utilize social media.

Online Calendars: To plan events and share them with friends and family, use online calendars such as Google Calendar. This facilitates the planning of calls, meetings, and visits.

Apps for Wellness and Health

Fitness Apps: To keep active and healthy, use fitness apps. You can participate in virtual exercise sessions with friends using a number of applications, giving you a shared fitness experience.

Apps for mental health: You may manage stress and preserve your mental health by using apps like Calm and Headspace, which include mindfulness training and meditation.

Telehealth Services: Make use of telehealth services to obtain advice and treatment from the comfort of your home. This can be particularly useful for routine check-ups and non-emergency medical advice.

Careful planning and a proactive strategy for preserving social ties and community involvement are essential to creating a supportive retirement community. Relocating to a retirement community has several benefits, such as improved safety, easy access to services, and social contact. Selecting the ideal retirement community requires careful consideration of your goals and preferences as well as an understanding of the various community kinds.

Maintaining relationships with loved ones and friends is crucial for a happy retirement. Strong relationships are maintained by open communication, regular contact, and active involvement in family activities. Creating new connections through online forums, clubs, and neighborhood events can broaden your social circle and improve your retirement experience.

Using social media, video calls, and applications for health and wellness can all help you stay involved and connected even when you're physically far away. You can have a happy and active retirement by fostering a supportive environment and keeping up strong social ties.

Chapter 19

Participating in Community Service

Retirement is a chance to contribute to the community and significantly improve the lives of others. This chapter looks at ways retirees can volunteer, the advantages of becoming involved in the community, and how to identify meaningful ways to give back.

Opportunities for Retirees to Volunteer
Regional Nonprofits

Food Banks and Shelters: Offer meals and support to underprivileged individuals and families by volunteering at your neighborhood food banks or homeless shelters.

Senior Centers: A lot of senior centers invite volunteers to help with events, activities, and programs aimed at elderly citizens.

Environmental Organizations: Participate in environmental organizations that prioritize sustainability, cleanup, and conservation efforts.

Animal Shelters: Provide care for animals, help with adoptions, and promote animal welfare programs by volunteering at animal shelters or rescue groups.

Academic Establishments

Schools and Libraries: Volunteer your time and skills to support educational institutions by planning instructional activities, helping with literacy initiatives, or tutoring children.

Universities and Colleges: A lot of universities and colleges provide volunteer programs that let retired people work as advisors, mentor students, or take part in research projects.

Medical Care and Well-Being

Hospitals & Clinics: Offer patients consolation and support, help staff with administrative duties, or act as a patient advocate by volunteering at hospitals, clinics, or healthcare facilities.

Health Education Programs: Participate in health education initiatives by organizing workshops, running support groups, or endorsing health awareness campaigns in your community.

Organizations that Perform Community Service

Lions Clubs and Rotary Clubs: Get involved in humanitarian efforts and community service projects by joining service groups like Lions Clubs International or Rotary International.

Disaster Relief Organizations: Offer your aid during emergencies, natural disasters, or humanitarian crises by volunteering with disaster relief organizations.

Community Involvement Benefits
A feeling of fulfillment and purpose

Making a Difference: Retirees who volunteer can support worthwhile projects with their time, expertise, and resources, which helps them feel fulfilled and purposeful.

Profound Impact: Retirees can positively influence others' lives and contribute to addressing urgent social, environmental, and health-related issues.

Relationships and Social Connections

Developing Relationships: Volunteering offers chances to socialize, make new friends, and get in touch with people who have similar interests and values.

Community Engagement: Taking an active part in the community keeps seniors engaged and connected while also lowering feelings of isolation and loneliness.

Advantages for Mental and Physical Health

Active Lifestyle: Engaging in physical activities while volunteering, such as gardening, mentoring, or attending community events, can improve one's general health and well-being.

Mental Stimulation: Social interaction and meaningful activity excite the mind and advance cognitive performance, which may lower the risk of cognitive decline.

Individual Development and Progress

Learning Opportunities: Through training courses, leadership positions, or exposure to novel situations, volunteering provides chances for individuals to advance themselves and acquire new skills.

Sense of success: Reaching objectives, conquering obstacles, and realizing the results of your work can give you a sense of success and enhance your confidence.

Discovering Valuable Methods for Participation
Examine Your Own Interests and Ideals

Determine Passions: When looking into volunteer activities, take your values, interests, and passions into account. Select causes that share your values and that you can relate to.

Evaluate Experience and Skills: To ascertain how you can have the most impact, evaluate your experience, knowledge, and prior accomplishments. Whether it'sevent organizing, fundraising, or mentoring, play to your strengths and leave a lasting impression.

Look up Local Businesses and Openings

Examine Your Options: Find out about local volunteer possibilities by conducting research on nonprofits, community organizations, and service providers.

Get in touch with organizations: To find out about volunteer opportunities, future initiatives, and volunteer criteria, get in touch with groups that interest you. Find out more about their goals, initiatives, and present requirements.

Begin Small and Gain Speed

Trial Period: To get a feel for what kinds of volunteer work you love best, start with short-term or project-based commitments.

Experience Evaluation: Consider your volunteer experiences and identify what went well and what needs improvement. Adapt your strategy in light of comments and lessons discovered.

Remain Dedicated and Adaptable

Consistent Engagement: To sustain momentum and create enduring connections with organizations and communities, make a commitment to volunteering on a regular basis and follow through on your promises.

Adapt to Changing Needs: Remain adaptable and receptive to new chances as they present themselves. Over time, volunteer work may change, so be flexible and sensitive to new demands and objectives.

Chapter 20

A Guide to Preparing for Retirement

A number of considerations, such as healthcare requirements, financial stability, and lifestyle choices, must be carefully planned for and taken into account when preparing for retirement. Ten actions are provided in this chapter to assist retirees in preparing for this significant life shift.

Choose Your Retirement Expenses

Establish Priorities: Think about your beliefs, passions, and retirement objectives. Think about how you wish to use your time, whether it's traveling, pursuing hobbies, volunteering, or spending time with family.

Create a Retirement Vision: Make a Retirement Vision Board or Written Plan: Describe your goals and desires in a written plan that reflects your ideal retirement lifestyle.

Examine Your Dream Retirement Lifestyle

Lifestyle Preferences: Take into account your inclinations with relation to neighborhood amenities, housing, location, and temperature. Decide if you would rather live in an urban, suburban, or rural area and if you would like to move, downsize, or remain in your existing residence.

Social and Recreational Activities: Consider your favorite pastimes and events and how you might fit them into your retirement plan. Think about enrolling in classes, groups, or organizations that share your interests.

Make a plan for your present and future medical needs.

Assess Health Status: Taking into account your age, medical history, and family history, assess your present state of health and project your future healthcare needs.

Examine Your alternatives for Healthcare: Examine your alternatives for healthcare as a retiree, such as Medicare, supplemental insurance, and long-term care. Recognize the standards for eligibility, prices, and coverage.

Calculate Your Retirement Costs

Budgeting Process: Make a detailed budget that details all of the costs you expect to incur in retirement, such as housing, healthcare, groceries, transportation, entertainment, and other miscellaneous expenses.

Take Inflation Into Account: When projecting future costs, take inflation into account to make sure that your retirement funds and other sources of income can support rising costs over time.

Choose Your Place of Residence

Location Considerations: When choosing a retirement community, take into account a variety of criteria, including cost of living, accessibility to friends and family, medical facilities, and recreational opportunities.

Investigate Your Housing Options: Investigate your housing options, such as staying put, moving to a retirement community, downsizing to a smaller house or condo, or moving to a different state or city.

Create a Plan for Retirement Income

Determine Your Retirement Income Sources: Determine the sources of your retirement income, such as investment portfolios, annuities, Social Security benefits, pensions, and retirement savings accounts (such as 401(k) and IRA).

Establish a Withdrawal Strategy: Plan how you will access your investments and retirement funds. Take into account elements like long-term viability, investment risk, and tax ramifications.

Guard Your Investments and Assets

Insurance Coverage: Examine your insurance policies, including those for property and liability, life, health, and long-term care. Make sure you have enough insurance to safeguard your possessions and reduce dangers.

Estate Planning: Draft an updated estate plan that outlines your preferences for healthcare directives, end-of-life care, and asset distribution. To make sure that your plan is thorough and compliant with the law, think about collaborating with an estate planning attorney.

Optimize Tax Efficiency and Retirement Benefits

Maximize Social Security Benefits: Recognize the guidelines and available options for filing for Social Security benefits, as well as how early or late retirement would affect benefit levels.

Tax Planning Strategies: Learn about tax-saving techniques, charitable giving, and Roth conversions to reduce your retirement income tax liability.

Get Ready for Needs for Long-Term Care

Long-Term Care Planning: Create a strategy for dealing with the needs for long-term care, taking into account possible expenses, arrangements for providing care, and ways to pay for it.

Examine the advantages of long-term care insurance as a way to safeguard your assets and guarantee that you will have access to high-quality care in the case of a disability or chronic disease.

Regularly review and update your retirement plan

Establish a regular review and update process for your retirement plan. This should ideally be done once a year or whenever there are major changes in your life.

Adapt to Changing Circumstances: Keep an eye out for modifications to your health, lifestyle, finances, or the state of the market, and alter your plan accordingly.

Retirement planning necessitates thorough planning, deliberate thought, and proactive decision-making. Retirees can lay a strong foundation for a safe, rewarding, and pleasurable retirement lifestyle by adhering to these ten steps and attending to important retirement readiness issues. Retirees can negotiate the complexity of retirement with confidence and peace of mind by being proactive now and preparing ahead for things like calculating spending, deciding on retirement priorities, and scheduling healthcare requirements.

Chapter 21

Important Questions for Baby Boomers Approaching Retirement

When Baby Boomers get closer to retirement, it's important to evaluate how prepared they are for this big change in their lives. This chapter examines important issues for Baby Boomers to think about when they approach retirement, with an emphasis on long-term care planning, financial readiness, and preserving independence and standard of living.

Evaluating Preparedness for Finances
Do My Investments and Savings Enough?

To find out if your retirement savings and investment portfolios will support the kind of lifestyle you want in retirement, assess them.

Take into account variables like chance of longevity, inflation, and medical expenses when determining whether your finances are adequate.

Have I Created a Plan for Sustainable Retirement Income?

Examine your retirement income sources, such as annuities, pensions, Social Security, and withdrawals from investments.

Create a withdrawal plan that strikes a balance between your need for income and the safety of your investments and savings.

Do I Have Enough Money to Handle Potential Risks?

Determine your retirement's possible financial risks, including those related to market volatility, longevity risk, medical costs, and unforeseen crises.

Create backup plans and risk-reduction techniques to protect your finances and adjust to evolving conditions.

Assessing Long-Term Care Programs
Have My Needs for Long-Term Care Been Considered?

Analyze your preferences and needs for long-term care while taking your health, family history, and aspirations for your lifestyle into account.

Examine your alternatives for paying for long-term care, such as Medicaid planning, long-term care insurance, and self-funding techniques.

Do I Already Have a Complete Estate Plan?

Examine all of your estate planning documents, such as advance directives, powers of attorney, wills, and trusts.

Make sure that the decisions you make about healthcare, wealth distribution, and legacy planning are reflected in your estate plan.

Have I Talked to My Family About Long-Term Care Planning?

Start having discussions with family members regarding end-of-life care, assisted living, and caregiving choices as part of your long-term care planning.

Think about how decisions for long-term care may affect relationships, family dynamics, and financial obligations.

Sustaining Self-sufficiency and Life Quality

What Actions Can I Take in Retirement to Preserve My Independence?

Determine ways to be independent and autonomous as you get older, such as continuing your physical activity, participating in social events, and making use of local resources.

Examine your alternatives for aging in place, such as technology-enabled solutions, supportive services, and home adaptations.

How Do I Develop a Meaningful and Satisfying Retirement Lifestyle?

Think about your beliefs, passions, and interests to find retirement-related hobbies and endeavors that fulfill you.

To keep involved and in touch with people, look into options for volunteer work, personal development, and ongoing education.

Which Tools and Services Are Available to Improve Life Quality?

Look into senior programs, support groups, and community-based options that can offer help, company, and advocacy.

To get companionship and emotional support, create a network of social ties with friends, family, and local groups.

Conclusion

Baby Boomers should approach this new stage of life with hope, readiness, and fortitude as they set out on their retirement adventure. This chapter emphasizes the value of continuing to be aware, proactive, and empowered in your retirement planning as a means of providing a final reflection on the major ideas and insights covered throughout the guide.

Accepting the Transition into Retirement

A major turning point in a person's life is retirement, which signifies leaving the workforce and beginning a new phase of independence, travel, and self-discovery. Retirement gives chances for personal development, fulfillment, and enjoyment even while it may also present difficulties and uncertainty.

Remaining Knowledgeable and Active

Making wise judgments and adjusting to changing circumstances requires staying up to date on the newest retirement planning trends, innovations, and resources. Baby Boomers have the power to take charge of their entire well-being, health, and financial stability by continuing to be proactive and involved in the retirement planning process.

Anticipating a Secure and Fulfilling Future

Baby Boomers should approach retirement with a sense of purpose, confidence, and optimism as they anticipate their golden years. Baby Boomers can design a retirement lifestyle that aligns with their values, objectives, and aspirations by utilizing their experiences, talents, and hobbies.

In summary, retirement is a journey rather than a destination, one that offers a wealth of chances for happiness, progress, and connection. Baby Boomers can successfully traverse the challenges of retirement by embracing this journey with openness, resilience, and determination. This will pave the way for a safe and rewarding future.

www.ingramcontent.com/pod-product-compliance
Lightning Source LLC
Chambersburg PA
CBHW071503220526
45472CB00003B/902